WHY I KILLED MY BROTHER

ZAVANE

COPYRIGHT

DEDICATION

This book is dedicated to my brother, Umoja Nia Augustus Spencer

December 3, 1972 - February 5, 1995.

The boy whom when I first met him, was the most beautiful baby I had ever laid eyes on. His dark smooth skin and curly hair only added to his big dark eyes. He looked different than my other brother and me, and to a young girl, his differences offered hope.

Not only were his looks different but I'd soon learn that his personality would differ also. He was a happy baby and grew up to be an even happier young man. He didn't carry the burdens like our other brother Jake and I did. He was carefree and always maintained a balanced demeanor. I don't recall seeing him angry very often and even if he was, it didn't last long. He would go right back to being the well-mannered, happy-go-lucky man he was known to be.

He was a quiet one, observing more than he spoke but when he spoke it was as if his words were smiling at you. He was very direct when communicating his likes and dislikes, but he was never rude. In fact, it didn't appear to bother him one way or the other, whether you liked what he said or not. He placed his importance on telling you his truth, not so much on how you received it. And like me, most received his words without resentment or disdain.

His passion for motor-cross made him one of the best in Bermuda, but it didn't make him arrogant or boastful He was humble and it was impossible not to love him.

Nia hadn't brought a girl home or introduced anyone as his girlfriend but from what I hear, he was a lover boy. Apparently, there was always more than one girl at any given time. This I can believe wholeheartedly. He really was easy on the eyes.

He was the best uncle to his niece and nephew. He didn't adorn them with gifts but instead could be found spending quality time with them often.

He had aspirations of going to college. He worked hard to make that happen but sadly wouldn't experience the fruits of his labor.

His life would be cut short just months before he was due to go.

I can only imagine the man he would be today had he lived. I can imagine him being an awesome son, brother, husband and father.

I can imagine him holding our family together in ways unique to him that would speak to the meanings of his names; Umoja (Unity and Nia (With a Purpose).

Missing him is not an option, because remembering him is a vital part of our very existence.

Zavane

PROLOGUE

It had been 23 years since the incident and although this was the first formal intervention, there had already been lots of informal ones before.

There were five of us in the small living room waiting for Jake: Randy the counselor, Daddy, Mama, Danez and me Zavane. The room was the exact same as when Nana had lived there 20 years ago. Facing the entrance door was the floral couch and tucked in each corner were two matching floral chairs.

My eyes went right to the piano, and I tried to recall a time when someone sat there and played a tune. Daddy was a musician and so was his brother, Uncle Grady, but for the life of me I couldn't remember either of them ever playing it, although Nana used to play sometimes.

I sat on the right side of the couch next to Daddy and the large stand with the family portraits against the wall close to me caught my attention. I gazed at each shelf starting at the top, taking in every item displayed. It was as if I was being taken down memory lane. There were portraits of Nana's children with their families, both of Daddy's brothers and their families and even more of my aunt and her family. She was the only girl out of three boys and if I had to guess by the number of photographs of my aunt and her family, I would be correct in my assumption that she was the favorite. Other than one or two of Uncle Grady, our family had the least number of photos displayed.

There weren't any portraits of my family together, not one. There were a few individual pictures of Daddy and each of his children, but that was it. This wasn't my first time seeing these pictures, but it was the first time I had noticed the disparity.

Shame on you Nana, I thought. *We were a family.*

I looked over to see where Mama was, and she had taken the chair directly across from the couch right next to the door. Danez sat on the left side of Daddy who had to shift to the center of the three-seater couch; and even though it sagged in the middle, it didn't seem to bother him. I moved closer to the corner so they could have a bit more space.

Mama and the counselor were engaged in small talk, as was Danez and Daddy. I was doing what I always did, observing. I scanned everyone, taking note of their expressions, whether their legs were crossed and how they held their hands.

All the seats were taken and I wondered where Jake would sit. There was space for another chair next to Mama, but Danez must've read my mind because he got up to place a chair from the kitchen there for Jake.

Bob Marley blasted from Jake's house next door.

Mama glanced towards where he lived and sighed. "Does he know we're here?" she asked of no one in particular.

Danez looked at his watch. "We still have a few more minutes."

Mama mumbled something and it was clear that she was frustrated, especially since we could hear Jake singing, as if he hadn't a care in the world.

Daddy was still making small talk. I was sure he heard Jake singing too, but Daddy was a patient man. It was completely in his nature to ignore Jake's antics and act like everything was fine. He appeared hopeful about the meeting, thanking us all for taking the time to show up.

Danez sat quietly although he did respond to Daddy's question by saying he was fine and filled him in on what was going on in his life.

Randy jumped right in and asked each of us how we were doing. He then briefly explained what the process would be once Jake arrived.

I found myself concentrating more on Mama's mood. I was curious about what she was thinking. In my mind she was the key to any possibility of a resolution or of Jake agreeing to go into rehab.

Jake and I were hugely influenced by her. She controlled us at levels she may or may not have been aware of and we were always trying to please her. The look on her face told me she was disappointed; probably thinking that she was wasting her time. Mama always had something to do and no matter what that was, to her it would be time spent wisely and way better than waiting on anyone.

A few minutes later, Jake arrived as casually as if it was a normal family get-together. He'd been drinking. He always drank, but one never knew if he'd be happy or angry. Today, based on his singing, he was happy.

The counselor started by explaining to Jake why we were all there: that we were concerned about him, that we needed him to become sober and that we were all prepared to take turns telling him why.

The room was set: Daddy, Danez and me facing Mama, Jake and Randy, and for a split second I thought about moving to sit next to Mama. The dynamics felt off. I felt sad and wanted to show my loyalty and support for her as she sat facing her ex-husband and his outside child. It just didn't feel right that I was there with the two of them. Hell, she was my mother for god's sake.

But I didn't move.

Daddy, who had been holding his head in his hands, cleared his throat and rubbed his palms together. "Look Jake, you know I love you. We all love you." His voice now quivering, he paused and continued. "I know you've been through some bad things in your life but it's time for a change. I've stood by you and supported you as much as I can but I'm sick now and I don't know how much longer I have left here. I want to see things get better but that's all on you. You have to do your part. You have got to stop drinking."

Daddy's eyes started to water and he stopped talking to wipe them with the back of his hand. His hands were huge and my eyes were glued to his move-ments. He was becoming emotional, but he also had a stern look on his face, like he was about to knock somebody out.

"Can you please just do this for you? For *me*?" he continued. "I'm tired of the fights, the drunken tirades, the instability and uncertainty of it all." With tears streaming down his face, he repeated, "I don't know how much longer I have left. I'm sick and you've got to get better."

How intense, I thought. *This is practically his last request.*

Daddy had prostate cancer and was going away for radiation treatment in Canada soon. He had received the diagnosis years earlier but hadn't agreed to any medical treatment as he was still seeking confirmation that the diagnosis was correct. His denial took him all the way to Cuba, only to have the doctors there confirm that his original diagnosis was correct.

Mama couldn't hide her disgust at what seemed like a pitiful plea from Daddy. It was no secret that she blamed him for everything that had happened. She wore her disgust like a Ruby Woo MAC lipstick.

She exhaled her famous sigh and went right for the jugular. "You're tired?" Directing her question at Daddy but not waiting for a response, she turned towards Jake and continued, "Everybody's tired. We've tried and I don't know what else you want us to do. You've lost your children, you're barely holding onto your job and it's just time you grew up.

We can't handle it any longer. You have to go to rehab. You can't do this on your own and if you don't go, I won't help you because I can't do this with you anymore. I've done everything I can and I'm not sure what more you expect from me.

"What do you want?" she continued, glaring. "Do you want to get better, or do you just expect everyone to take care of you? What do you want for your life?" She was done talking but continued staring at Jake as if expecting an answer. Her authoritative tone boomed across the room and her body was stiff, but Jake didn't seem fazed at all by anything Mama had just said, which I found very interesting because Mama's tactic hadn't changed much over the years. Whenever she wanted us to do something her way it always started with accusations or blame and then she'd guilt us by telling us how our actions or choices affected her.

Then there was the question that made us think we actually had a choice in the matter, but we rarely did. Typically, we always felt really bad and just did whatever it was she wanted us to do. At some point, Jake and I completely disregarded her dramatic demands and that always ended with a beating. Jake didn't seem to fear her like he used to, like I still did sometimes.

This shit was impressive. My brother, the alcoholic, was manning up to the one woman who had, up until now, controlled his entire life. Had he finally realized that he was the only person who should have control over his destiny? There were times when I told him he was the one giving Mama the power over him because he relied on her for everything. I had tried to empower him and make him believe that he was more than capable of running his life, but he had so much guilt for what he believed he had done *to her*, and he always went right back to her when he found himself in a bind.

Maybe this would have been the perfect time for him to succumb to her request, but this was a decision he had to make for himself and not for anyone else, especially not Mama.

Jake sat nodding his head, but he had the strangest smirk on his face. His shoulders were low and loose and he remained unresponsive to Mama's comments. He displayed a very nonchalant demeanor, and I couldn't figure out what that look on his face meant.

Danez had been sitting quietly and seemed genuinely interested in what Daddy and Mama had to say. Now he was looking perplexed. I wondered if he was thinking what I was: that this was not going well.

He cleared his throat and began speaking.

"Jake, we love you man, and we really want you to get better. We're here to help you. I'm here for you and you only need to let me know how I can be of assistance."

Danez was our half-brother and Daddy's son. Although they knew each other, he and Jake didn't have much of a brotherly relationship at the time, so it made perfect sense that he kept it brief.

It was my turn and to be honest, I wasn't sure I wanted to say anything.

I am Zavane, the eldest child of three children born to Daddy and Mama and the only girl. Jake was the middle child and Nia the youngest. I had long felt that I was different and from a young age, I noticed I could feel what others were feeling in ways I couldn't describe.

Those feelings always had me trying to make things better for everyone, especially my family. I was the ultimate people pleaser but so very miserable inside. For some reason I thought that if they felt better, I would too.

There in Daddy's living room I was a different person than I had been. I saw no need to keep the peace but rather to let the meeting play out in its entirety and as it was meant to. I was concerned but not in a way that had me feeling the need to control the outcome. Besides, we had a trained counselor in the room.

I sat there in my feelings, trying to fill the gaps which had been left by everything that hadn't yet been said. No one had talked about the elephant in the room. No one had offered forgiveness for Jake's horrendous actions years ago. No one had even talked about *why* he drank every day, and to me the whole intervention seemed like a shit-show and a waste of time.

I knew the expectation was that I'd echo what our parents had said, but I was frustrated by their lack of bravado and instead I looked at Jake for a few seconds before saying, "I love you, but you have to love yourself. You know I'm here for you."

A wave of silence washed across the room and I dropped my head wondering if, yet again, I had failed my brother. This would be the second time I had been asked to formally help him and both times I chose to do the bare minimum.

Daddy and Danez sat upright eager to hear Jake's response, and Mama actually looked a bit hopeful. She squirmed in her chair and was smoothing out her dress. She seemed to be getting ready for what was next.

"Thanks for sharing, everyone," Randy said, breaking up the uncomfortable silence. "Jake, do you understand what everyone has said? Is there anything you would like to say?"

Jake grinned like he was about to put on the performance of his life.

I smiled. It was good to see him happy about being able to express how he felt, sans the drama that usually accompanied his outbursts.

"Listen everybody," he said. "I appreciate you all being concerned about me. You can call me a drunk, hell that's what I am. I know you need your money." He directed this comment to Daddy. He was months behind on his rent, which was also Daddy's mortgage payment. "I know you don't need the stress since you're sick and I get that, but you all have to understand that I accept who I am. You may not like it, but I'm good. I like me. I'm happy being this way and if you all are finished saying what you have to say, I'm about to bounce."

After asking everyone if they were certain that they had nothing else to say, he thanked Randy for showing up, shook his hand and left.

A few minutes later we could hear Jake singing along to Bob Marley's *'Who the Cap Fit'* as it blared on his boom box.

How fitting, I thought.

"Ok everyone," Randy said offering an empathetic smile. "All's not lost as there are things that each of you can do to effect the change you want to see. But first let me advise you that this is how these interventions typically go. What happened today is normal. Jake has made it clear that he is happy with who he is, and what normally happens next is that the remaining family members start to argue and blame each other for not getting the anticipated response from their loved one. From speaking to each of you, I know you aren't happy with how he chooses to live, so what I am going to suggest is that you all work on breaking the codependent ties you have with Jake and put your energy into yourselves. I'm happy to speak to you individually if you're not clear on what I am suggesting. He's not ready for change but it'll be helpful for each of you to work on creating healthier lifestyle interactions with him."

Mama's screams cut him off and she sat on the edge of her chair as if she was ready to pounce on Daddy at any moment. "Okay, I hope you see what you've done! I'm so sick of this shit!" Her expression was sour, and she stared at him coldly.

Daddy's small beady eyes were wide open, and he threw his hands the air. "Rain, come on. Don't do this now." Daddy continued to sit looking sad, filled with hopelessness, dread and maybe even guilt.

Mama scowled and Daddy sat shaking his head in disbelief.

Randy attempted to continue with his advice, but no one was listening.

Danez and I locked eyes and with unspoken words, agreed it was time to go. We both stood.

I thanked Randy for his efforts, told him I'd be in contact with him for the individual assistance he had offered and patted Daddy on his shoulders. "Everything will eventually work out," I whispered into his ear. "Don't stress." Then I looked over at Mama. She was glaring at me and once more, I felt as if I was betraying her by showing care and concern for Daddy.

"Are you leaving?" she asked.

"Yeah," I replied. "I'm ready."

Mama and I had driven to Daddy's house together and I knew the drive home would either be a shouting match or eerily quiet. Either one would be very uncomfortable.

I felt for my parents, but I understood my brother. I knew that he hadn't forgiven himself for what he'd done. The counseling he received at Westgate Correctional Facility only made him angrier and he swore off any type of psychological assistance since being released.

Alcohol numbed the memories, the ones he remembered every day of his life. Alcohol was his medicine and while I agreed with the others that he'd need consistent therapy in a facility, I knew that ultimately the decision would have to be his if he was to have any success taming his demons. And he had once again made his decision.

I loved them all, but it didn't appear that they loved themselves. I don't think *any* of us did or even knew how to. This was the conclusion I had come to many years earlier after watching Mama blame everyone for everything and not acknowledging the role she might have played in any of it.

Daddy thought he could fix people by being understanding and nice, but the truth was he lived in an era that was long gone. Things had changed and he talked as if life was still the way he remembered it being back in his day.

"When I was a young man, I wouldn't have dare spoken to my parents that way. I listened to my mother and did what she said."

This was something we had all heard him say but it was so irrelevant now.

Neither of them had let go of the past and they both actually believed they still had control over their now 40-something-year-old son and could make him change his ways. Neither of them had tried to change *their* ways. They bore so much anger and guilt, and it was my assessment that if they loved themselves, they would've sought help, did the work to become healthy and whole and maybe then they might've had a chance of helping Jake.

I had tried to convince both to get counseling and shared my thoughts of ways for self-improvement, but it had been met with disdain. Daddy had returned to the church and believed that God would help him heal. Mama also believed in a helping God. I only wondered where the hell he was and when he was going to show up and do something.

Years ago, when Jake was still incarcerated, I had arranged for Mama to meet with the psychologist I was seeing at the time. The meeting lasted all of 10 minutes. He started out by asking Mama a series of questions, which she answered easily but when he asked her about her marriage to Daddy, and more specifically, why she stayed in a relationship in which she was unhappy, everything changed.

Mama sat upright in her chair and responded with a certainty that she had done something good. "I stayed for the children's sake."

He nodded his head as if in agreement and asked, "How do you feel that worked out for all of you?"

Mama did not like this question. Her nostrils flared and her eyes bulged as she looked directly at him. At that moment, Mama held her chin high, stood up and stomped out.

The psychologist and I sat there for a few minutes in silence.

Initially it hadn't been clear that Mama wasn't ready to have that conversation but now it was.

The one thing Mama and Daddy both agreed on the occasions I had tried to convince them to get help was that I thought I was better than everyone else. Daddy's favorite response was, "Who do you think you are?"

Eventually, I gave up and helping them was a battle I had long ago conceded.

It wasn't my war.

Suffer not the children
Lest the sins of the parents befall them
For they are not equipped for such
things
Their births an act of love...
Not war.

My parents were very popular and who they were in public was very different from who they were at home. They removed their superpower suits and became two different people.

Mama worked all the time. Her days were spent between three different jobs and Daddy was an entrepreneur of sorts. He was also an entertainer who played in a steel pan band and a commercial fisherman. In addition to that, he had some type of business with foreigners, what exactly I didn't know, but it required him to travel frequently.

At home, my parents fought long ugly fights. They argued about the bills, other women and the lifestyle that Daddy had chosen to live. He loved fancy cars, fast boats and traveling. When he wasn't traveling, there was always some strange man visiting. They would stay with us and if they didn't, they were given access to our house, as if they were a part of our family.

I was a young girl and in addition to school, my responsibilities included taking care of my brothers. I prepared dinner, ironed our school clothes and most times, settled them in for the night. I was the only girl and the eldest, so I guess it made sense that I would assume Mama's role while she was working.

It was the strange men that Daddy trusted so much that made me uncomfortable. They were in and out of the house constantly. One of them took to visiting our bedroom and I would pretend to be sleeping while he stood there staring at me. After I was certain he was gone, I'd wake up my brothers, carrying the youngest one, and make my way to one of the neighboring houses asking if we could stay until our parents returned. The first few times this happened I stayed, but I couldn't go to sleep until either Mama or Daddy came through the door. I would be exhausted the next day and found it difficult to get the boys sorted in the mornings and to school on time. Going to a neighbor's house allowed me to get some sleep. Besides, it was scary having these strange men come in and out of the house when neither of my parents were home. I just didn't feel safe.

On the nights that I took the boys and left, the three of us would find ourselves being awakened at some wee hour in the morning by one of the neighbors telling us our parents had called and we could go back home.

———

I started leaving my island home at a very young age. When I was ten years old, I was off to St. Kitts. Some of Papa's relatives had come to Bermuda for a visit and although we had just met, I asked – no I *begged* my aunt and uncle to take me with them.

I had no idea where St. Kitts was or what these people were like to live with. I just knew I wanted to go, and Mama was all too happy to let me.

It was decided that Ma, my maternal grandmother, would travel with me and after all the arrangements had been finalized, we left. I don't recall being upset that none of my parents could accompany me. Ma was the perfect companion. She was the person I felt most comfortable with anyway and I didn't doubt for a minute that she would be the one who missed me the most. I knew I would miss her dearly, so it was perfect to be able to spend this time with her.

———

I settled in nicely. Our house in St. Kitts had a backyard that was full of the most beautiful trees I had ever seen. I fell in love with trees there. We also had a garden full of vegetables and fruits, all in the confines of our backyard. Papa had gardens in Bermuda but his were big ones with one main crop. This garden was a lot smaller and more personable. I liked my new home and the quaint backyard.

Life there was simple. School, church and trips to the mountains and the sugar cane factory were the weekly events. I wasn't the only child in the household. They had three daughters and a son. I was the youngest but almost the same age as their youngest. It was amazing having older cousins who were more like siblings. With all my responsibilities back home, I had come to resent being the eldest. Here, I was the youngest. I was both relieved and happy.

I didn't feel like Cinderella there. Chores were divided equally between all of us, and I willingly adapted to the routine.

My year in St. Kitts taught me that there were families who got along, were happy and that a simple life was what I wanted when I had my own family. We would take trips, eat meals and pray together. This would be the epitome of my newfound definition of family.

Mama and Daddy came for a visit. The local Holiday Inn hotel had just been built and Daddy's band, contracted by the hotel chain, came down to perform for the grand opening.

The Holiday Inn in St. Kitts was only one of the stops for the band. The band was on a tour of the islands, maybe spending a day or two at each, so our visit together was brief.

I returned home after a year and a half in St. Kitts and re-enrolled into my old school, Elliott. I'm not even sure why I had to return. I think maybe my extensive travel between St. Kitts and Bermuda became too expensive for my parents. I don't even know who made the decision or why and I had no choice but to do what I was told.

I was in my final year of elementary school when Jake had an accident in gym class. Another student had been sent to my class to collect me and initially I was irritated that I was being pulled out, but when I got to the gym, I knew that he was not in a good way.

Jake was lying down on a mat in the gymnasium, curled up in a ball and crying. He winced in pain when anyone tried to touch him. The ladies in the office said they had called my parents as well as an ambulance. Jake had broken his neck. He had landed on it after attempting a gymnastics jump.

We visited him in the hospital. They had placed a cast on him that looked like a space suit. From his head to his waist, he was covered in a hard white plaster with only his face and arms out. He was so uncomfortable when he first came home but he got used to his cast quite quickly. If he had an itch, Mama had a stretched-out wire hanger that we would use to scratch it for him. He was in that cast for nine long months. He was a trooper though, and at seven years old, handled the drastic change to his life like a champ.

I was in high school for just two years before I found myself wanting to leave my island home again. Things hadn't changed much between Mama and Daddy.

The boys had grown nicely and were both involved in motor-cross riding and doing very well. They loved the sport. Both of them became top contenders. Between practice and race days, they kept busy. I went back to filling the gaps left by Mama's busy schedule and on the weekends, I was pretty much home alone. Daddy and the boys would be at Coney Island for motor-cross training or out fishing on Daddy's boat.

Mama would be working and I would be home prepping dinner, washing and ironing clothes and cleaning house.

One particular Sunday, I wanted to go to the corner store and get some candy. My uncle had just returned Daddy's pedal bike, so I thought I could take a quick ride to the store get some and be back home before anyone called to check on me.

Uncle Grady was a special one. He was Daddy's younger brother and had done some jail time for importation of weed a few years prior. When he was released, he went on a vacation to Jamaica. Upon his return, the customs officials found marijuana in his bags, but he denied knowing anything about it. The truth, as I had heard from family members, was that he had been set up and Uncle Grady did not want to go back to jail.

At some point between being arrested and processed, he changed. My guess is that the thought of another lengthy jail sentence was more than he could bear and he *lost it*. He lost any semblance of normalcy and went 'crazy in his head,' so instead of sending him to jail, they sent him to the psychiatric hospital in Bermuda – St. Brendan's.

In the years prior to any of this, Uncle Grady was an entertainer performing in the hotels and clubs on the island. When I was a little girl, he often reminded me of *Mr. T.* He always had gold chains hanging from his neck and was always dressed in the finest of clothes while driving fancy sports cars. I was proud of my uncle with his swagger and brilliant smile. It was so cool having a celebrity in the family.

After being released from St. Brendan's a shell of the person I used to know, he came to live in an apartment around the corner and attached to our house. I wasn't afraid of him even though he still acted crazy from time to time. What I didn't know this one Sunday morning was that he and Daddy had previously spoken about the pedal bike. Daddy had demanded the return of it and he did, but not before he'd loosened the bolts on the front wheel. I just wanted candy and the bike being returned meant I didn't have to walk to the store.

I got dressed and was excited that I'd be able to treat myself in just a few minutes. It would be the highlight of my day and my own little secret. Smiling, I hopped on the bike and was on my way.

I did not make it to the corner store. All I remembered was cruising off the hill from our house, the breeze in my face and feeling very happy.

I woke up in an ambulance on the way to the hospital. I tried asking the EMTs what had happened, but they encouraged me to lie still. I remembered where I was supposed to be and in an instant, the focus of my fear shifted. I was no longer worried about what had happened to me but more about how Mama would react to my attempt to leave the house. I started hyperventilating and the nurse did her best to calm me down.

Mama was going to be mad. I had no idea how badly I was hurt but that wasn't on my mind. I was trying to figure out what to say to Mama once she found out.

I was still in the emergency department when Mama came and *mad* didn't begin to describe her anger. She looked at me and grimaced.

I immediately started to cry.

Not being a sensitive woman, Mama said she couldn't care less about my tears.

She glared at me with piercing eyes as though I were a demon. "What the hell are you crying for? You did this to yourself!" she hissed through seething fangs.

I turned away from her and stared at the wall.

After surgery I learned that they had sewn 54 stitches in my face. The loosened front bike wheel had disconnected from the bike frame as I cruised down the hill and I slammed into the pavement face first. Knocked unconscious, I lay in the street until a neighbor drove by and found me. I had been lucky, they said, because I had just missed hitting the electricity pole, which of course, could've been much worse.

I was released from the hospital and because I couldn't be trusted to stay home and obey the rules, I now had to sit at Mama's job while she worked. Her job was in the city and it was always busy. I pleaded to stay home. I didn't want to be seen like this, but she wasn't having any of it, and so I sat in her restaurant looking like a freak show for everyone who came in.

I can't recall how many times Mama told her customers my story, *her* way – how I was a disobedient child and that I did not deserve their sympathy.

To me, at the age of 16, she was just mean, and I didn't like her at all. She was an angry woman. Of course, at the time I had no idea what she was going through. All I knew was that Mama didn't like me very much and I often thought of other ways to receive the love and attention I only ever wanted from her.

The following summer school break, the boys and I spent most of our time at Mama's new restaurant.

There were two guest houses in the area, and I was always meeting visitors to the island.

The constant stream of visitors afforded me the opportunity to meet people. Some even allowed me to go and live with them overseas.

I started living in Malden Massachusetts and moved to Dorchester Boston mid-term while attending Malden High School.

Before that school year had ended, I moved to Stamford Connecticut to live with my aunt to finish my high school education there. I had been searching for the experience I had in St. Kitts and hadn't found it. I figured it was in my best interest to stay with family if I was to ever feel that type of security again.

Months later, after my arrival in Stamford, my parents decided to divorce. They had visited Connecticut often and it didn't take long to realize that their visits and I were being used as a pre-cursor to the final show down, the court hearing.

Daddy would come and buy me whatever I wanted and soon after, Mama would be in Connecticut asking for a transcript of our conversations and the receipts from all the stuff he'd bought me. She said it was important for her case against him.

Two months before school was ending, Mama showed up without warning, took me out of school and flew me back to Bermuda for an appointment with her lawyer, R. Merrill. Mr. Merrill needed me to tell him everything that I could remember about Daddy's visits to me.

I told him I was interested in becoming a lawyer, but he disregarded my comment as if it was a passing fantasy and said, "Yes, well that's very nice, but let's get on with the business at hand."

I just wanted to be seen but preparing for Mama's slam dunk case against Daddy was the priority. Her plan was to take everything from him, as if it would make up for all of the suffering she attributed to him. The plan was to take the house and his boat and of course, he would have to pay a huge amount of money as atonement for all his wrongdoings.

For a quick moment, I thought about Daddy, wondering if he'd feel betrayed by what I had told the lawyer, but Mr. Merrill told me that whatever I said would be held in confidence.

I left the appointment having changed my mind about becoming a lawyer. They didn't seem to want to know the whole truth about a situation before representing someone and that didn't sit well with me.

I probably wouldn't be a good lawyer anyway. Shoot, will I even finish high school?

The thoughts passed quickly because Mama was satisfied and in a good mood, and nothing took precedence over me enjoying this rare moment with her. These moments were uncommon and I reveled in them.

The divorce took years to be finalized. Mama fought tooth and nail to get what she felt she deserved from Daddy. She didn't get the house, but she had succeeded in getting his boat, the boat that was his love, his life.

Daddy was heartbroken.

Jake and Nia were too, and they asked me why she had done it. I knew she was being vengeful, but I told them I didn't know.

Daddy's 54-foot boat was placed in what became its graveyard.

Mama kept saying she was getting it fixed up and we would get to use it again but that never happened. The boat sat there and rotted.

Daddy went on to start his own restaurant and eventually purchased another boat. This one was much smaller than the first, but it made him just as happy to be out on the water again.

I wasn't able to return to Connecticut in time to complete the school year but was able to go back and finish by enrolling in summer school. Afterwards, I returned to Bermuda hoping that the worst had passed for my family and things would be different for all of us. I was tired of being away from family and friends.

Once you start running my child
Don't stop until you reach the finish line
What if there's no finish line in sight
Mama?
Then you just keep running
Until you can't anymore

CHAPTER 2

I was working for the airlines when I got the call. I went upstairs to the first-class lounge where I could hear better and have a cigarette while I listened to the person on the other end.

Daddy had been arrested. There had been a drug bust and he and a few others had been arrested as well. It had something to do with containers of beer and marijuana and apparently, lots of it.

I was confused. Nothing was making sense.

Daddy was staying at the hotel with his lady friend, and he hadn't been to his restaurant, The Fish Bite, all weekend. He wasn't scheduled to leave the hotel for a few more days. I tried calling a few people who I thought might know something more, but no one answered.

Bermuda is a small island and word travels fast. In less than half an hour, people started asking me questions.

I had no answers for them.

My phone started blowing up and if it wasn't a family member, I didn't answer. The rest were just pokey-ass people who would be nowhere to be found when the shit really hit the fan.

I called my brothers. We needed to talk about this current situation. They were the only people I trusted.

I was now in what Daddy called *Mama Mode*. I had to get him a lawyer and create a plan, but first I needed information and I knew that my brothers would know more than I did about what was really going on.

They both agreed to meet at my house that evening and they were there when I arrived.

Jake was visibly upset, pacing back and forth.

Nia was shockingly calm. He didn't seem stressed at all.

I asked them what they knew; did they think that Daddy was in big trouble?

Just then, I remembered a conversation I had with Daddy a few weeks ago:

He was distant and very quiet, and I cornered him in the storeroom at the restaurant one evening and asked him what was going on. I told him that he seemed different. I wanted to know if I had done anything to upset him. Everything at the restaurant was going well and it bothered me seeing him like this.

He told me to sit down on one of the boxes then he sat quietly for a few minutes holding his head in his hands. "I'm ok, just a bit distracted and there's nothing wrong, but I need you to get something – really. You need to understand that everything is not about you! If someone doesn't speak to you one morning when they usually do, or if another person doesn't talk to you when they normally do, do not automatically think it's about you. You just don't know what people have on their minds. You'll never know what it is they are dealing with. I need you to not take it personally because most times it has nothing to do with you. You haven't done anything to upset me. In fact, I appreciate you and the way you are handling the restaurant."

With that said, he stood up to leave.

Watching him, I asked, "So, what's got you distracted?"

Daddy was smiling and shaking his head as if he was wondering what he was going to do with me. As he walked out of the storeroom he responded. "Zavane, I could be smuggling diamonds. I could be smuggling diamonds."

I sat there for a few more minutes. I knew he wasn't telling me everything and we both knew I wouldn't leave it alone.

When I went back into the restaurant he was talking and laughing with a customer, but his behavior seemed veiled to me. What was he hiding? What was he trying to protect me from? These questions and others consumed me as I vowed to pay closer attention to his every move from then on.

The boys and I met in my back yard. What we had heard happened was pretty much the same. Neither of them seemed to know anything more than what I had already been told.

Jake stood with his arms crossed and didn't have much to say. I noticed his gaze was fixed on Nia the entire time we were in the yard. I didn't give it much thought because he and Nia were always fussing about something.

We discussed securing a lawyer and I agreed to keep them updated with any progress I made in doing so.

Jake hopped the fence that separated his apartment from my cottage and I went back inside, leaving Nia in the back yard.

I was in my kitchen making a cup of tea when I heard Jake shouting at Nia, "You need to do the right thing! This is fucked up."

I went to the back door and could see Nia and he didn't seem disturbed at all as he walked towards the gate leaving my house. "Ya boy's gonna be cool," he said as he passed by me. "They can't put this on him. Calm down! Everything is going to be alright."

Jake didn't respond.

"Where are you going?" I asked Nia. I was now on the front porch trying to keep up with him as he continued walking.

Nia didn't turn around to acknowledge my question. He simply threw his hands up in the air as if to indicate he didn't know and walked away, but just as he approached the main road I heard him mumble, "For a walk."

They held Daddy for 72 hours for questioning. He was released on police bail and on September 7, he was charged with importing marijuana and handling a controlled substance, namely marijuana, with intent to supply. I had retained the services of B. Robles, the most talked about lawyer at the time. He had a reputation for winning his cases.

After bail was secured, we went straight to Robles' office where we discussed the charges and a potential game plan. We decided to hire a Queen's Council (aka a QC). The lawyer recommended this, as these charges could result in a possible ten year or more sentence and Daddy maintained his innocence. Even though he didn't have to prove his innocence and the proof of guilt lay with the prosecution, it was in his best interest to secure the topmost counsel we could afford.

I handed over my bank book with my savings balance as security for the QC. He would fly in from the UK for the actual case which could be some time away, but we had to secure his services ASAP.

Life would go back to normal in the interim and we would meet with the lawyer as needed. Daddy went to the police station three times a week as a required condition of his bail. All we could do now was to wait.

I was in constant Mama Mode. I attended each appointment with the lawyer, trying to put the pieces together as Daddy answered the questions put to him.

Something was not adding up.

Daddy's story didn't change. "I was at the hotel when I got a call that a shipment of beer had arrived, but I hadn't ordered any beer. Of course, I went right to our warehouse because I didn't know what the heck was going on. Then the next thing I knew, the place was flooded with police and the rest is history. I hadn't even opened any of the boxes. I had no idea the boxes were stacked with weed."

The shipment had come from New Jersey. I remembered one of Daddy's business partners had a brother who lived there.

I got his number and called him.

It was the shortest telephone conversation I've ever had.

"Who is this? Zavane? Don't call this number again!" the man on the other end of the phone said and then he hung up.

I hadn't trusted that man with the green eyes when I first met him.

I knew he had something to do with this mysterious shipment of beer but more importantly, the drugs stashed inside. I had only met him once, but instinctively I knew that he was suspect.

The talk subsided and life got back to normal. We got through the Christmas holiday and welcomed the New Year. The holidays meant that Daddy would be making cassava pie, a traditional island cuisine. We would have our customary family dinner with everyone bringing a dish; everyone except Jake and Nia, that is. They just showed up, ate and hung around until it was time for them to find their way to some friend's house they'd been invited to.

Christmas dinner was going to be at Ma's house and although Mama and Daddy were divorced, Daddy was welcomed. He still had a good relationship with both Ma and Papa.

Mama was always cordial, and the day was always filled with lots of conversation and laughter and that year was no different. Maybe I was the only one who noticed my brothers, who although cordial, did not say much to each other.

I was certain that all of us were hoping for a year different from the previous and for a positive outcome for Daddy when he went to trial.

Parents living as if they've got time
Encouraging their children
To always be more
Children dying instead
Their growth stunted by fear

CHAPTER 3

On February 5, 1995, my telephone rang at around 3 AM. It was Mama and she was screaming, saying we needed to get to the hospital.

I jumped up, dressed and off we went.

Mama told me to put my blinkers on and to drive faster. That was all she said.

The entire drive I was thinking, *What the fuck could've happened now?* I knew it had to be one of my brothers, but I had no idea, nor could I have even imagined in my wildest dreams what awaited us at the hospital.

The admissions nurse recognized Mama when we walked in. She ushered us to follow her to the emergency room.

When death calls he doesn't say much
He just whispers
Come

CHAPTER 4

The hospital was packed inside and out. There were people everywhere. I tried to avoid direct eye contact with anyone but recognized the faces of a few of my brothers' friends in the waiting room area.

Just as we were being escorted to the private section of the emergency room, I overheard one of them say, "Man that was fucked up of Jake!"

I wondered what the hell my brother could have done.

"Nia didn't deserve that," I heard someone else say.

My phone had been blowing up with calls, but I didn't answer until I saw a call from Nia's godmother, Aunt Shaz.

"Hi Zavane, how's your mama? She called me to say that Nia has been stabbed. Is he ok?"

"Umm, we're at the hospital now," I responded, confused as to what she was talking about. "No one has said anything to us yet and we're just waiting. If you want to come by, call me when you're here and I'll meet you at the emergency room entrance." I hung up.

So, Mama knew he had been stabbed, and based on what I had overheard; Jake had been the one who stabbed him. Feeling confused and extremely worried, I started to focus on what everyone else was doing, trying to silence my thoughts by watching them.

I hoped the situation wasn't as bad as I was imagining.

Inside the emergency room's private quarters, Daddy was punching the wall. Mama went right into crisis mode, asking him – no, *screaming* at him, "Oday, what happened?"

A nurse came and escorted us into an even more private room and asked that we wait for the doctor to come and talk to us.

Daddy didn't go into the room with us. He went outside using the side door, the one used when a patient arrived at the hospital via an ambulance.

We were left there for what seemed like eternity. I couldn't sit still. I wandered back to the less private area and after careful observation, realized that the room my brother was in was right across from the nurses' station. The only separation was a curtain pulled across the doorway. I leaned against the wall outside the room and listened. I heard a man say, "We're losing him. We need more blood now!" This time he was yelling. I knew it wasn't good.

Now I was pacing back and forth in the small corridor, not wanting to go back into the room with Mama.

Nurses were now rushing in and out of the room. I was now sitting, head bowed; looking up every time I heard movement.

I felt a hand on my shoulder. It was Daddy, he had come back inside.

"Any update?" he asked.

I just shook my head indicating no.

I hadn't noticed prior to Daddy returning, but the Trauma Room was really quiet now.

"Excuse me; can I get you to return to the family room now please?" Asked the nurse who had been on the desk when we first arrived.

"The doctor will be right in to speak with you," she said as she turned to walk towards the private family room.

Daddy followed her. I, instead, went screaming through the waiting room, out the automatic doors and collapsed onto a concrete bench. I held myself, somehow knowing that Nia had succumbed to his injuries. I just knew what the doctor was going to say.

No one came after me. I sat shaking uncontrollably and cried. Then out of nowhere, a sudden calm came over me. I looked up but there was nothing but dark sky. I felt a warm air engulf me and it was calming. Instinctively I knew I had to get up, go back inside and deal with whatever was awaiting me.

As I had presumed, Nia had died. Two police officers whom I recognized were now there. One was holding Daddy. I ascertained that he was trying to restrain him from further damaging the wall and himself, the other was just standing there. The latter seemed relieved when he saw me and immediately asked if I could go with them to collect Jake for questioning.

I was terrified at that thought. "Umm, hell no!" I responded. I still wasn't clear on what he had to do with any of this.

Jake had displayed some behaviors in the past. He had been violent before. He was aggressive and scary at times, and I wasn't sure what to expect, so I declined the offer to accompany them.

The officers confirmed that he was at home and said they were leaving to pick him up. They asked if I would go again, but I felt I needed to stay where I was. The officers left and once they were gone, I regretted my decision.

I would never know what happened in those moments. I instantly started worrying about Jake, how he was being treated and how he would react – if he would be safe.

If I had set my emotions aside, I might have willingly gone with those officers. To this very day I still believe that had I gone that night, things might be different for him; for all of us.

Back in the family room, the doctor was offering Mama a sedative which she declined, and I gathered that Nia had been stabbed and had lost too much blood. He had lost most of it prior to getting to the hospital. They had tried to replace it, but his body had gone into hypovolemic shock due to the volume of blood lost and they were unable to save him.

They were cleaning him up and we would be able to see him in a few minutes.

I couldn't sit still and didn't stay in any one space for too long. I wandered about, but didn't stray too far from Mama and Daddy.

We hadn't had the chance to call anyone yet, but the word was already out there. Family members and close friends were flooding into the emergency waiting room.

The reception nurse came in and asked for one of us to come out and speak with them.

The waiting room had almost emptied of all the people who had been there earlier. Everyone there now was familiar to me. I told them that we were waiting to see Nia and if they wanted to, they could wait for us.

"We shouldn't be much longer," I said walking back towards the private area of the emergency room.

Seeing Nia on that bed lifeless and clean, he looked like he was sleeping. Viewing his dead body was the reality of the situation none of us could even begin to comprehend. We were all wondering how this could've happened.

I searched his body for signs of a stabbing and when Mama noticed what I was doing, she reminded me that the doctor said it was in his neck. They had placed a piece of tape there.

I guess I missed that information while I was on the bench outside.

His head was positioned in such a way that one would not immediately notice it.

I moved his head and removed the tape. Mama gasped, but I continued and when I finally had the tape off, all that was visible was a pinky finger sized cut. I was confused! For the life of me, I couldn't understand how someone could die from such a small invasion.

What the fuck was going on?

I made Mama look at it and for a few seconds I had distracted her from the untimely death of her youngest son, as I gave her something else to think about. Mama left the room in search of the doctor who could make what we'd just seen sensible for us.

After looking over Nia for a few minutes more, I left the room.

Mama was standing at the nurses' desk waiting for the doctor who we could see was in the small back office.

He came and suggested we walk back to the family room. Once there, he explained that Nia's jugular vein and carotid artery on the left side of his neck had been cut.

"The artery is about 1.5 inches below the surface of the skin," he said. "Once severed, and unfortunately in your loved one's case, it results in death rather quickly."

I remembered the family members who were outside waiting for us and went back out to the waiting room. More had arrived and those that wanted to, were given the option of viewing him.

Nia's godmother Shaz had come, and I took her right to the private room to be with Mama. I needed her to be there for her because honestly, I had no idea how I was going to console her. I had no words of comfort and touching wasn't our thing. We didn't hug on a normal day, and it had become such a foreign thing for us to do.

Hours had passed and there wasn't anything else we could do at the hospital. We hadn't forgotten Jake, but we didn't know what to do about him. Standing in the hospital parking lot we agreed that we should go to the police station. It was almost five o'clock in the morning and we had nothing else to do. I don't think any of us wanted to go home, or maybe it was that none of us knew what it was we should do in that moment, so the police station seemed the best option. We knew for certain where Nia was – dead in the morgue and we wanted to make sure Jake was alright; I wondered if the officers would tell him that Nia had died.

We didn't know if he was being held at the police headquarters which was in a different parish from the actual police station. We decided to go to the station because it was manned 24/7 and we knew we would be able to speak to the officer on duty there.

The officer at the desk checked on the case after we gave him Jake's name and quickly came back to advise us that we wouldn't be able to see him. We were told to secure the services of a lawyer who would be able to get more information.

As soon as we stepped outside Daddy called Mr. Robles who assured him that he would ring the station and go there as soon as he could. Daddy said that he would be in touch with us as soon as he knew something.

We all walked to our separate vehicles looking like zombies.

Daddy hugged me before he left to go home. He looked over at Mama who was standing next to my car and said, "Rain, take it easy."

Mama just nodded her acknowledgement.

Mama and I drove home in silence. I'm sure we were both immersed in our own thoughts.

I didn't think our lives could get any worse and that Daddy's situation was the worst we'd have to deal with, but this was the trump card none of us knew existed. Had we known, we would've burned it. Family feuds were one thing, but this fight had been taken to another level.

I didn't know what to do. I knew I hadn't grasped the magnitude of the situation. In my mind, I was in a nightmare. It all seemed surreal. There was part of me that kept thinking I would wake up and it would all be over.

After Mama and I arrived back home we gathered at my grandparents' house, which was between Mama's and mine. Daybreak arrived soon after we had. People started showing up at Ma's front door just after 9 AM. We used the living room as the meeting room and with each new arrival, the story of the night before developed.

One young lady showed up with her mom and recounted how she called for the ambulance. When it still hadn't arrived after some time, she decided to put Nia in her car and take him to the hospital herself. She remembered hearing his breathing become labored as she reached the Crow Lane Roundabout, just a few minutes away from the hospital.

She told us about the fight inside the club. Jake was fighting a mutual friend of his and Nia's and Nia stepped in to separate them; however, it seemed as if Jake had taken offence, feeling that Nia was taking the other guy's side. Jake was removed from the club by security for being drunk and disorderly.

She continued by saying that maybe an hour so later, they were leaving the club when they saw Jake sitting across the street on his bike. He and Nia looked at each other but no words were exchanged. She asked Nia if he was ok, and he said that he was. Apparently, they turned to walk in the opposite direction to her car when Jake crossed the street and approached Nia aggressively. She jumped out of their way.

Jake grabbed Nia by his shirt. He was screaming that Nia was fucked up and that he would pay. Nia tried to get away from him, she said. The scuffle didn't last long.

She didn't recall seeing a knife but in what seemed like a matter of seconds, Nia was on the ground with blood gushing from his neck. There wasn't much of a fight between the two, she repeated. Nia pushed Jake away, turned around and collapsed. No one knew that he had been stabbed until they saw the blood. When she looked across the street, Jake was gone.

It was then I remembered Daddy's and my interaction with the police officers the night before:

"Have either of you seen or heard from Jake?" the officer asked.

"Earlier, before I got the call from the hospital he stopped by the restaurant. He was crying and told me that he was sorry. I didn't get a chance to question him," Daddy said, "because he rode off when I went to get closer to him."

It was mayhem after that with a crowd forming. All she wanted was for an ambulance to come and get Nia to the hospital. She had called 911 repeatedly, but there was no response to her calls for help.

Court Street was in the area we referred to as the 'Back of Town'. This was the area where drug dealers and prostitutes could be found. It was also the area where one could be sure to encounter black-on-black crime.

Then, just as she was about to leave, she told us that she thought she might be pregnant with Nia's child.

We exchanged numbers and agreed that we would speak soon.

Jah, who was a neighborhood friend, was already crying when he showed up. He hugged Mama tightly and sat on the couch wiping his face.

"Moms, I didn't know it would go this far," he said. "I mean, I saw Jake and ya boy scuffling, but when I saw Nia intervene, I just thought everything was cool."

"Why were they fighting?" Mama asked.

"I don't know. I just thought it was some petty shit. Jake was pretty drunk though. Next thing I knew, they were fighting each other and that's when I went to try and separate them, but at the same time, the security officers came and told Jake that he had to leave. I asked Nia if he was ok. He said he was and everything else was cool, or so I thought. I just thought the scuffle between them would blow over." He started crying again.

Mama went over and hugged him and they sat there for a while, holding each other.

Many others showed up at Ma's house. Some came to offer their condolences while others came to share what they had witnessed with hopes of filling the gaps.

It was all too much –different versions of the same story. This was typical in Bermuda; people exaggerated situations all the time. There could be five people at the same incident and you were guaranteed to get five different accounts of it. I could only imagine what the police would have to go through.

For us, it only muddled things even more. We hadn't been there and no matter what we were told, the versions told to us would always be the facts of others and not our own. We had lost one son at the hands of the other based on what had been communicated to us. We weren't a drug cartel family. This wasn't supposed to happen and we didn't know how to deal with this, let alone know where to begin. We would all soon learn that there wasn't very much for us to do at all.

It was out of our hands.

They speak of a calm before the storm

I don't know that calm

I only know storms

My storms have names

I call them family

CHAPTER 5

Within 48 hours, Jake was being charged. No one had seen him since he'd been arrested, so showing up to court was twofold. We wanted to make sure he was ok and to hopefully provide bail so he could come home and tell us exactly what had happened.

The courtroom was packed with reporters, family members and random people. I noticed that there were lots of police officers and undercover agents. It felt like we didn't know the true magnitude of the situation.

There was a witness for the Crown, the son of the club owner where the fight had taken place. He told how Jake had been removed from the club for disorderly conduct and how a knife, which had been taken from him on his entry, was given back to him by security when he was ejected.

The voices in my head were saying, *"I'm sorry, did you just say that you gave a knife to a person you were ejecting from your club for being drunk and disorderly? They should lock you up!"*

The Royal Gazette front-page article on Thursday, February 9, 1995, read:

"Man charged with brother's murder
Despite highly-emotional pleas from his mother and lawyer, 25 –year-old Jake Cole was yesterday remanded in custody for the death of his younger brother."

The charge was murder and there was no bail. He was being remanded in custody until trial.

Mama's wails quieted the entire courthouse. "Please don't take my other son from me," she screamed.

I tried to make eye contact with Jake, but his head was in a bowed position and he didn't look up.

I went outside and waited for Mr. Robles to come out. I wanted to speak with him on both matters now at hand. Leaning against a wall, I started to relax in the breeze, but my body had other plans and started to shake uncontrollably.

A plain clothes police officer came up to me and suggested that I be taken to the hospital. He actually increased my awareness of what was happening. I knew I needed to stay in control of myself. I couldn't let go. There was too much I had to do and being taken care of wasn't an option. I had to stay in Mama Mode because everyone else around me was collapsing. Besides, all my life I had been groomed to take care of others and this situation required that I fulfill my duties.

Mr. Robles told us to come right to his office to discuss the court hearing. Daddy, Mama, Danez and I made the short walk and piled into his small office. We discussed timelines for a trial date, who we thought he could interview regarding the events that led to that day's court appearance and when he would go to the prison to speak with Jake directly.

He advised us to call the prison to find out when we could visit as well.

We gave him the names and contact details of the people who had visited and who we knew were there that night.

"I'm sure they will talk to you," I added.

Mr. Robles reminded us that these types of situations are usually met with people not wanting to be involved but that he would reach out to them and hope for the best.

I asked about Daddy's case, and he mentioned that interestingly he'd heard that Nia had traveled to New Jersey the week before the drugs arrived in Bermuda. He wanted us to bring Nia's passport for concrete evidence that he had actually travelled to the United States.

Mama flipped. She started cursing and saying that we were trying to mar her deceased son's name. How could we? She wailed.

Suddenly, a light bulb went off in my head. I realized that this was something we would have to discuss when she wasn't around. I suggested this to the others, aware that she didn't hear what I was saying since she was so caught up in her grief and anger.

I stood to leave and tapped Mama on the shoulder signaling that we were. We left Danez and Daddy in the office with Mr. Robles.

I thought briefly about what the lawyer had said and wondered if the three of them were discussing it further now that Mama wasn't there. I spoke to both of them later that day and neither of them mentioned it, so I assumed it was a non-issue.

Mentally I went through my to-do list. I had to call the prison as well as finalize funeral arrangements. The funeral was going to be in five days, there really wasn't much time.

Feeling loss as if it were mines to own
Overwhelming guilt
As if it were the seed I had sown
Oh blame, rear not your hideous head
I already have an abundance of regret
Wishing it were me instead

CHAPTER 6

Mama was the core of our family, the one with the strength when we had none; the one who had the answers to all the problems we had ever encountered. She would pull it all together and leave us in awe every time. During times like these, she amazed me, but I was also filled with resentment because of how she had treated me. Loving Mama had been a balancing act and that shit was hard.

On the drive home, it came to me that she had let go, just like I had threatened to do outside the court-house. I didn't know if there was any returning from that place once you succumbed to it and I didn't want to find out. I sure as fuck wished she hadn't because who the hell was going to pull this mess together now?

I remembered her strength and wondered if we'd ever see that side of her again. I believe that was the first time in my life seeing that side of her. She had never been vulnerable. Maybe she thought it was a sign of weakness. This woman managed her own restaurant and had helped her father with his construction business. Hell, she even drove the damn trucks picking up sand and concrete for the work sites! She was diligent and expected the same of me.

She didn't seem to have the same expectations of my brothers though. She babied them, especially Nia. Everyone knew he was her favorite.

She taught me to treat them the same way. I became their second mother as a young girl. I watched them while she worked at night, made sure they were bathed and had eaten, and I resented every minute of it. I promised myself that when I became a mother it would be the complete opposite of what I had experienced.

I was silly and young then and had no concept of what kind of life she had lived and the circumstances that led her to becoming this way. Life would soon teach me the error of my thinking.

Mama had been a beautiful woman. She sang in an all-girl group and was once offered an opportunity to go to New York to audition and quite possibly start a career over there. Her parents declined the offer and she settled into a life of wife, mother and provider. I'm not sure if they expected lots from her or if she had just decided that she would be the best at whatever she set her mind to do.

But damn, she was tough and I received the brunt of her toughness. I remember one parent-teacher meeting at my high school. I was passing every class except one and that woman yelled at me like there was no tomorrow. Needless to say, I was embarrassed. We were in the school's gymnasium and everyone could hear what she was saying. I just couldn't understand how 9 out of 10 was not considered good. I often wondered what *would* be good enough for her and as the psyche would have it, I tried to please her, whether I was in her presence or not, and it was almost always not quite good enough.

Papa had built a very successful construction company. Mama's brothers were groomed to take over the business but they both died before Papa. They were alcoholics. My uncles worked with Papa for many years and their drinking had cost him dearly.

They were foremen who were left in charge of job sites, but more than once they had become distracted by the drink and made costly errors. They had caused Papa to lose money time and time again.

Papa was a patient man, but he was also very tough and serious about his work. It wasn't long before neither of them was allowed to work with him and Mama happily filled the void. She was a Daddy's Girl. It appeared that she didn't get along with Ma very well and preferred to spend her time close to her daddy, even if it was on a construction site.

Papa adored her and she had him wrapped around her fingers, all of them. He would give her whatever she wanted.

Mama didn't seem to like her brothers very much. They were "idiots" and addicted to alcohol, so it really aggravated her that Ma would even consider trying to assist them. She didn't view alcoholism as a disease but a choice, a rather stupid one.

Ma was very patient and loving with her boys. She would do whatever she could to try and help them. She had taken in both them and their children on occasion and these acts of kindness made Mama very angry.

From her perspective, they didn't deserve help. A swift kick in the ass maybe or even a slap upside the head would do, but the ultimate goal would be them being disowned and not ever thought of again. She always said that the day Ma and Papa died she'd put them out of the house and they wouldn't be welcomed around there anymore. She didn't get a chance to act on her intentions because both brothers predeceased their parents.

Mama was not one to withhold how she felt about her brothers. She was very vocal about them and to them.

I remember wondering if I would be the same way with my brothers. I talked to Ma often. I wanted to understand what had happened between the three of them. I didn't want the relationship I had with my brothers to resemble that of Mama and her brothers in any way.

Our families were too much alike and I was sure that I was the one who felt most like what I thought her brothers must've felt like. She treated the boys like the best things to have happened to her and me? Well, I was her real-life Cinderella and she was more like my stepmom than my mother. I considered myself a burden with no idea of what I had done to become one.

I was ugly!

That had to be it. I was red skinned with blonde hair and she was dark with long black hair. She was beautiful. She must have been extremely embarrassed by me.

The things kids think when they don't feel loved.

Not once did I consider that our family structures weren't the only things that were similar. I wasn't aware of, or knew how Ma had treated Mama when she was a little girl. Ma treated me with such love and care that I wouldn't have even considered that Mama might be treating me the way she had been treated.

But something in me believed that my being a Daddy's Girl and both boys being spoiled by Mama were not just coincidences.

She's such a daddy's girl
Aren't they so cute?
But she's my mama too I wailed
My cries went unheard
My voice was on mute

CHAPTER 7

The visitors started to come less frequently, and we had to sort out visitation to the prison and plan a funeral.

On the night after the incident, I walked Mama down the hill to her house. We had just left Ma's house and she was going to get some rest. I stood on the other side of her door and she locked it. I turned the handle to make sure it was indeed locked before I left.

The next day, Mama asked me if I remember checking her door to ensure it was locked.

"Yes," I replied. "Why, what happened?"

Mama told me how, approximately an hour later, she heard something banging. She went to investigate and found her door wide open pounding against the frame.

Strange, I thought. I knew I'd checked and it was locked.

We chose to believe that Nia had returned home. His spirit had returned home.

———————

Papa's nephew owned a funeral home. My uncle and his sons came to Ma and Papa's house and walked us through the process.

Mama was numb. She didn't say much, and her eyes were dark and distant.

We started planning for the church service. Everyone had suggestions but Mama remained eerily quiet.

I was worried that Nia's funeral was going to be a mess. From selecting the casket to organizing the speakers and singers, it didn't seem as if we knew what the hell we were doing.

Mama was staying at Ma's and Papa's house now. No one wanted her to be alone in the apartment she and Nia had shared up until his untimely death.

We'd spend hours trying to plan his funeral and it must have been when we all left on any given day that she did the impossible. With only days before the funeral, Mama showed us her plans and holy shit; she had planned the whole damn thing. She had arranged for choirs, individual singers, speakers and pallbearers. She had even confirmed the church and the minister who would lead the ceremony. I had picked a suit from Daddy's closet for Nia to wear and although she hadn't seen it, she was ok with that being done.

Nia's body had been moved to the funeral home and I asked my cousins if I could dress him. They said it was cool, as long as I thought I could handle it.

I assured them that I would be ok.

Although we hadn't discussed it we all knew that this funeral would be the largest event we had ever planned and that all eyes would be on each and every one of us. What had been dubbed as the "Cain and Abel" murder was the first of its kind in Bermuda. It had been covered by all of the news media outlets and was being talked about by just about everyone on the island. We were a very proud family, and this was way more difficult than Daddy's drug charges. People already talked about Mama and Daddy's shenanigans but now they were talking about their children's.

We only went where we had to – the lawyer's office and the funeral home. Everything else we needed somehow found its way to us. People were generous and helpful. They cooked food and held us up in prayer as well.

I had friends who constantly checked on me and assisted with my children while I spent at least two hours at Ma's house every night. My circle was small, but they were very supportive.

With so much going on, I had neglected to sit my children down and tell them what had happened. They were seven and four at the time. The day after the incident; Monday, February 6th, I didn't send them to school. After being in the house most of the day, I allowed them to go out and play with their friends later that afternoon.

They were only outside for a few minutes when both of them ran back to the house.

"Mama, mama!" Both of them were calling me louder than usual.

"Dwayne said Uncle Nia is dead. Is that true?" the eldest asked. Her uncle was special to her. He spoiled her lots and he always found time to be with her.

They both looked at me wanting confirmation that the neighbor's son was telling tales. Before I could answer her, she inched closer to me and grabbed my shirt and whispered, "He said Uncle Jake killed him. Why Mama, why?"

I took the kids in their bedroom. They were so young and I had no idea what I was supposed to say. Little did I know, whatever I said would prepare me for what I would have to tell both of them years later. I confirmed that what they had been told was true. Yes, their uncle had gone to heaven, the place where the angels lived. I intentionally neglected answering the second part. I just told them that their Uncle Jake would be away for a little while, but they would see him again real soon.

We talked about heaven like we talked about Santa Claus. I was saying whatever I had to, to make them feel better. I finally left them lying in their beds crying softly.

I took a seat at the kitchen table and realized for the first time that I was alone. Both of my brothers were now physically absent and I felt emotionally abandoned. I wondered if this was how they had felt when I had left them.

The funeral was planned for Sunday, February 12th, but we still hadn't seen Jake, other than at the court hearing. All we knew was that he was being held in maximum security and wasn't allowed to have visitors yet.

Being in maximum security meant he only had one hour per day outside, so for twenty-three hours each day he was locked in a cell. I often wondered what he thought about during all that time. After inquiring, we were told we could send him reading material. We sent motor-cross magazines and a Bible. At least he was able to see the lawyer who reassured us that he was doing as well as could be expected.

Jake would be allowed to attend the funeral, albeit under heavy police protection. Apparently, there were threats of retaliation, from who we didn't know. Whoever they were, they must've been crazy to think that this family would stand by idly and see another son killed.

Such a daily mix of emotions became draining. I didn't know what the rest of the world was thinking but we didn't have anyone to hate for the death of our son, brother and grandson. Shoot, we didn't even know why it had happened. With the exception of what we'd been told, we still didn't know the truth. This was one of the few times we stood together firm and unshaken. We were all determined to do whatever it took to take care of Jake throughout what promised to be a very turbulent next few weeks, possibly years.

The suit I picked out for Nia was hideous and I don't know what I could've been thinking when I chose it. It was almost as if I saw it for the first time the day I went to the funeral home to dress him. It was suitable for an older man, but I reasoned that because he was so handsome, it wouldn't matter. Nia was dark skinned like Mama, and he had the warmest eyes. The blue checkered suit would look good on him.

He was laid out on the metal slab, eyes closed and looking like he was sleeping. I looked at him for a while. The hole in his neck was no longer visible. His skin, although now cold and hard, was still beautiful.

What a shame, I thought.

I removed the white sheet and decided to start from his feet and go up. I placed socks on his feet realizing just how heavy his limbs were – heavy and stiff.

Being lifeless was hard, cold and heavy.

It didn't take me long to realize that I was dressing his shell, that the person I had known was not here. He had been a really sweet guy with a warm personality.

I wondered where he had gone and where he was. I remembered Mama's account about the door banging after having locked it and I believed that he was home, safe and sound. Well, not him literally, but his spirit.

I'm not quite sure why, but I smiled and went about dressing him as if I were a painter painting a house. I wasn't sad anymore. It was as though I was prepping for a dress rehearsal and the main character had gone ghost, but I wasn't worried because I knew where he was.

My cousin came to assist with the finishing touches and advised me that once Nia was in the casket, they could fold and tuck the parts of the suit that were too big under him. He assured me that Nia would look fine. Even though the suit was too big, the blue looked good against his dark brown skin.

I looked him over from head to toe and tried to remember the last time I saw him dressed up in a suit. I remembered that it was at Danez's wedding and smiled at the memory. He was so debonair in his black tux that day. He was a charmer everyday but *that* day, he looked the part.

Then I thought of him in his motor-cross gear and considered that I could've dressed him in that, or any one of his sweat suits or jeans. I must have been holding my breath because I exhaled and told myself that he looked just fine.

He was dead and it was crazy that I was concerned with what he looked like. This is just the housing, I told myself and for some strange reason I thought about my house and how I would clean and not allow the children or their friends to come in and play.

My house was always clean but like Nia, empty. That would have to change. It was then that I decided a happy home was much better than a clean and empty one. The thought reminded me of my time spent in St. Kitts and my insides warmed.

The random thoughts that filled my mind baffled me when I took the time to analyze them. I didn't know why they came when they did. What I did know was I always learned something from them, no matter how arbitrary they seemed to be.

Who was I becoming, I wondered?

I sat in the room for a few more minutes, gathering the strength to go back outside. Being there in the cold room with Nia seemed much easier than being with everyone else, and part of me envied him. Being with death was easy. It was being with the living that I found difficult.

After death whispers, come
It is silent
It speaks no more
It leaves the noise to Life

CHAPTER 8

Westgate Correctional Facility had recently opened, replacing the former Casemates Naval Barracks. This brand-new facility was where Jake was being kept. I thought this was a good thing. At least he wasn't in that old dingy prison.

On our first visit to see him, Mama, Daddy and I had no idea what to expect. I figured they'd visited Uncle Grady at Casemates, the former prison, but this experience would be different.

After presenting our visitor passes and being searched, we walked through metal detectors and down a corridor. Not far from the security checkpoint, a metal door opened and we walked through.

The sound the door made when it closed scared me. I froze and looked back. This was my first experience being inside a prison and my very first insight of what it was like to be locked up. Straight ahead was another metal gate and although I could see it, the steps to reach it were countless.

Two more gates later, we arrived in the visiting room. It was almost full. There were men – lots of them – sitting at tables with family members or loved ones. I recognized a few people but was careful not to make eye contact.

I thought we would get to choose a table and I scanned the room for an empty one. Instead, we were led to a very small room with two chairs and a glass with holes in it. One chair was on the other side.

Two officers escorted Jake into the room and the door closed behind him. He didn't look at us right away and when he did; his eyes were red and swollen. He stole a glance at us then quickly hung his head.

I didn't say a word. Instead, I looked to my parents for guidance, but they looked just as clueless as me. Seeing them this way made me sad. This shit could not have been easy for them.

Mama asked Jake how he was doing. He mumbled something and started to cry.

I was standing, looking down at all of them and what I saw that day changed me. I didn't know these people. Mama and Daddy had become mutes right in front of my eyes. They were at a loss for words.

Jake appeared to be broken beyond repair. How could he be expected to know how to respond to the question?

I wished that my parents would start shouting at one another and that Jake would yell at them to shut up. I wished that my family would return to normal right there and then, that the glass would disappear and the orange jumpsuit Jake was wearing was instead blue; the color of his mechanic job issued ones.

The government may have been proud of the newly built facility, but now, having visited, I made a mental note to write someone in Department of Corrections a letter. They had missed some key components in constructing this stark white place. They had forgotten door stops so the gates wouldn't scare anyone when they arrived; rugs on the floor that added color to the all-grey rooms and cushions in the seats so that when you visited with a loved one you were comfortable. Yeah, they had forgotten a lot of things when putting this place together and I, for the life of me, couldn't understand how they expected anyone to ever call this a place of residence, even if it was only for a little while.

Daddy seemed to take it all in. He looked around at everything, often catching the eye of someone he knew. He had to have spoken to at least five people while we were there.

He appeared very interested in the facility. To my knowledge this was his first visit there as well, so I was surprised when I mentioned I had to go to the bathroom he was able to direct me.

Was it even possible for him to know what the future held in store for him?

Conversation with The Lord

The Lord: "Thou shalt not murder."
The People: Shall we kill him for his
transgression?
The Lord: "Not so; anyone who kills Cain will
suffer vengeance seven times over."
Me: Oh Lord, Jake is our Cain. Will you shield
him from death as well?
The Lord: My child, death is not punishment.
Losing your mind is.
Tend to his mind.

CHAPTER 9

The day before the funeral I showed up at the funeral home to have one more look at Nia. He was now in the cedar casket and the white lining surrounded him like clouds. The old suit really did look good on him.

The viewing would be that night and the curtains would be drawn, allowing everyone who attended to gaze upon his lifeless body. In hindsight I wished we had planned a private funeral, but it was way too late for that now.

I hadn't given any thought to what I would wear and wished I didn't have to. I didn't care what I looked like, but I knew that the others would. I couldn't show up looking disheveled, and as much as I was a mess inside no one could see that. More importantly, I couldn't *show* them that.

We all had to appear as if we had it together, like we always had, no matter what was going on. Our grief and confusion were ours alone and tonight the viewing was for all the others. This was their opportunity to express their grief and we would console them. We would appear strong and understanding.

They would expect us to be broken but they wouldn't see that. Not tonight. Not in this public place. We would reserve that for when we returned home. No, tonight we would be one or the other: consolers of the mourners or stoically quiet, but none of us would be emotional.

If there was any family member to be concerned about, it was Mama. Remembering that she had recently started taking medication, I knew that there would be no show of emotion from her either. She would sit quietly, seemingly void of feeling as she had been for the past two days.

Mama went to her doctor shortly after all of the planning had been done for the funeral and right before our first visit to see Jake. It doesn't seem she started taking them right away because her demeanor had only changed since our prison visit.

Death on display
And they line up
to see proof of death
They sign a book
to show proof of presence
They speak words of comfort
to a family who won't remember a thing they've
said
The only thing they're aware of
Is their loved one is dead

CHAPTER 10

The funeral was being held in the Hamilton Seventh Day Adventist Church hall. It had been suggested because it was anticipated that the church would be too small.

Mama, Ma, Papa and I arrived in the limo courtesy of the funeral home. Other than the parking spaces reserved for family, the parking lot was full. The streets outside the church building were lined with onlookers and the churchyard was full of people too.

I immediately became overwhelmed. I looked at Mama and she had a blank stare. She looked like a rag doll with her arms hanging loosely by her sides. I wondered if she even noticed the crowd.

The limo stopped and Daddy's ex-wife, Joslin, came up to the car and tapped on the window. I read her lips as she said, "I am so sorry."

I nodded as acceptance of her condolences.

I secretly wished we could've stayed in the limo, but we had to get out. They had positioned the car as close to the entrance of the hall as they could. I don't know how we made it inside the hall. My legs were wobbling as I walked. Mama walked in front of me with the assistance of her nephew from the funeral home.

They directed us upstairs to assemble with the rest of the family where we lined up and made the long walk to our seats.

People were still viewing Nia's corpse. Some were placing letters and cards inside his casket. This was very invasive to me. I wanted to go and close it myself. I couldn't imagine why they thought he would know what they were doing or be able to read what they had written.

We took our seats in the family section which was roped off and left three vacant seats in the front pew for Jake and two prison officers. I noticed lots of undercover officers in the hall as we walked in, but it wasn't until the casket had been closed that two prison officers walked him in from a side entrance.

There was a jacket over his hands, which gave me the impression that he was handcuffed. I was sitting two rows behind so I couldn't see his face. He kept his head in the bowed position for the most part and those who were sitting directly behind him would occasionally rub his shoulders lovingly, but he wouldn't look up. Jake sat a seat away from Mama and Daddy on the left side, with one prison officer between them and the other at the end of the pew.

The family section had grown ten-fold. There were visitors from overseas consisting of my brother's friends and family members we hadn't seen in years. We had received phone calls from a young Hispanic lady in New York. Her name was Sarena and she also said she was Nia's girlfriend. They had recently been together in New York and were in constant contact. They had plans to go to Florida to attend college in the fall.

I wasn't surprised by her revelations. My brother was a very free spirit who moved privately. You would see him one moment and in what seemed like the next, he was at the other end of the island or in another country. He came and went as he liked, and I recognized his need for freedom from the status quo. His need to keep moving reminded me of my earlier days of leaving. I had hoped that he would find a way out, but not like this. We knew of his plans to attend college later that year. He would be a mature student at 23 years old, but he was still young enough to attend, finish and create the life he desired. Some said that he was too old to be starting college at 23 – to hell with college. He was too young to be dead.

We sat quietly, waiting for the clergy to arrive on stage. Lost in my thoughts, I remembered when Nia was born. Jake and I were in school. Mama and Daddy came to the school with him in tow the day Mama was released from the hospital. We were called to the office and led to the front yard and there they were in Daddy's MG convertible. He was the most beautiful baby I had ever seen. His complexion was dark like Mama's and his head was covered with black silky hair.

Jake and I were both fair skinned like Daddy, "red-boned" as Daddy would describe it, proud of his Indian heritage. We had red skin with blonde hair, but Nia was different, dark and beautiful.

It was easy to see how he became Mama's favorite, thanks to Daddy's antics and both Jake and I resembling him. Nia gave her hope for something different.

The deacon announced my name, signaling that it was time for me to go on stage and read the obituary.

I stood, looked around and exited the row. One of Mama's friends, Sevon, stood also. He walked to the steps leading to the stage with me and whispered that he was going for support. I thanked him and we approached the pulpit.

I arranged my copy of the obituary and once again looked over the crowd of people. My gaze rested on Jake. I was willing him to look up and he did for a few seconds but lowered his head right after our eyes met.

Something came over me and I knew I wasn't going to read the obituary as planned.

I started speaking almost as if guided by another force.

I saw the confusion on people's faces as they tried to follow what I was saying within their copies of the obituary, but what I was saying wasn't there.

I didn't know Swahili, but when I opened my mouth, I started with our names in that dialect. I was just as shocked as the mourners' faces displayed they were.

I addressed the church. "Good afternoon, everyone. In the dialect of our Swahili brothers and sisters, *Wai-Zwu*, Jake's given name, means *strong boy*. *Nia* means *unity* and *Zavane*, *strong girl*. These names were not given in vain. They were not casually chosen, but rather, they were inspired by God. I'm not sure if my parents knew it at the time, but our names were not selected randomly by our godfather.

I'm not even sure if *he* knew the magnitude of gifting us with these names; that one day they would serve as a testament of who we had to be. Today, the meaning of our names serves as a reminder. Jake, my brother, as your name indicates, you are strong! I need you to remember that, especially now. Nia has paved the way for a *Unity* to move in our family as we have never known."

I was looking directly at Jake. I needed to know that he heard me. He looked up and for the first time since his arrest, I saw a sense of relief on his face.

"I know we are all gathered here to mourn the loss of our brother and it is without question that he was loved," I continued, "but he is gone. We who are left behind need your prayers and support. Jake needs your love and I ask that you show him mercy and let him know that he is not alone."

There was a resounding "Amen" from the mourners.

I paused and looked at Jake again, hoping he had heard their acknowledgement of support for him. He didn't look up this time. His head was bent and he was weeping, using the jacket that covered his hands to wipe his face.

"There will be lots of talk in the near future with court cases and news reports," I said, "but know this: Jake is family, and his family loves him, and we will not forsake him nor leave him. If you are a part of our family, let me hear the church say 'Amen'."

Once again there was a collective "Amen" from the mourners.

I said thank you and exited the stage, stopping briefly in front of Jake to rub his bowed head.

In that moment, I felt as if Nia's death would not be in vain, that it was part of a bigger plan, and although I had no idea how it would all unfold, I found some comfort in that knowing.

I finished, leaving the stage different than I was prior to going up.

Sevon had stayed and addressed the congregation. "Good afternoon church. On behalf of Rain, Oday and the entire Cole family, I would like to thank you for your well wishes and acts of kindness. As you can imagine this is a very trying time for the family. Continue to keep them in your prayers as they deal with what can only be called a tragedy."

As Sevon left the stage, the Seventh Day Adventist choir came on and sang the most beautiful song. I say beautiful because it felt peaceful when they were singing. I don't remember what they were singing, only how it made me feel.

After an opening prayer the minister spoke. His voice commanded attention from everyone in the hall.

"The book of Matthew tells us to judge not, lest ye be judged. For with what judgment ye judge, ye shall be judged."

I didn't know it at the time, but this would be one of two times a minister would modify his sermon based on spontaneous changes I would make to an obituary I was about to read.

The second would be at Daddy's funeral service.

We have wept and the night has been long
You said that joy cometh in the morning
Father
When will the morning come?
Your children are waiting

CHAPTER 11

After the sermon on forgiveness and a reminder of how God forbade anyone to harm Cain after he had killed his brother Abel, numerous tributes, choirs singing and soloists, we lined up to exit the church.

Jake was gone, taken out the side door he had been brought in earlier. This was quite a spectacle with all the trimmings of a real-life movie. Undercover police officers scattered throughout the church hall with prison officers on either side of Jake. I wasn't sure what they'd anticipated happening that warranted all this security. There seemed to be more people there now than I had remembered.

I was feeling conflicted and wasn't sure why. My emotions were all over the place and for some reason I felt like we were being judged by everyone. I started making direct eye contact with people I didn't even know, as if to let them know that I knew what they were thinking, that I knew that they were the enemy, and I wasn't afraid of them or their judgments. I was confused and angry. I was losing my composure and I had to get my shit together.

Just then, my cousin, the funeral director's son, approached me, put his arm around me and asked, "You ok, cuz?"

I looked at him dazed and he squeezed my shoulders before directing me to the limo Mama was already seated in.

The funeral procession to the graveyard was being led by a group of motor-cross riders and Nia's bike was on the truck in front of the hearse. Inside the car a Bob Marley tape was playing. *"Misty mornin' don't see no sun; I know you're out there somewhere having fun."*

I looked through the tinted windows for any semblance of the sun, but it was a gloomy day and like the song suggested, it was there, it just wasn't visible.

We arrived at Christ Church cemetery and were once again lined up to make our way to the grave. I wasn't sure how they would get the casket up the hill. Nia's final resting place was at the very top of the graveyard and I was a bit anxious.

The men took their places around the casket and were able to roll it until they got to the bottom of the hill, then they picked it up and began their trek. I stood back and watched but once I was satisfied that they would make it, I made my way to the open grave by another route. Having lost my spot in the procession, I found myself amongst mourners, people I didn't know.

I had a good vantage point and could see Mama, Daddy, Nia's two female friends and Ma and Papa. The pastor was front and center at the head of the grave and once the casket was in place, they began the Rite of Committal. The pallbearers were called to start lowering the casket and the wails began. Mama's was a low moan and Sarena was screaming in her native tongue, while the young lady who thought she was pregnant for Nia was sobbing loudly. All were being consoled by whoever was closest to them.

I looked at Ma and saw her wiping tears from her eyes. Daddy still looked like he was in shock, disbelief almost. He now had the same blank gaze as Mama had as his eyes followed the casket and his son down into his final resting place – the place where he would turn to ashes and dust and his casket would eventually rot, it was only a matter of time.

They lingered around the grave for a few minutes after the ministers had left. I had already found my way back to the parking area and lit a cigarette. Others who were leaving stopped and asked if I was ok and gave their condolences. I nodded saying, "Yes, thank you."

I saw my cousin Dave from the funeral home and went over to ask him if he had removed Nia's jewelry and other objects that had been placed in his casket. He said yes and mentioned that he also took a lock of his hair in case we wanted it. He would get them to me, he said. I was bewildered by the lock of hair but quickly reasoned that Mama would be happy with that.

I stood there looking at all the people, seemingly very present but my mind was on Jake. I wondered how he was feeling, *what* he was feeling.

Had he eaten?

Were they comforting him?

Was he ok?

All these questions ran through my mind and were probably heightened each time I'd see another undercover police officer.

Damn, they were even at the burial.

Apparently, there had been talk of gang members trying to 'take Jake out' at the graveyard. Rubbish, I thought. It was just people and their need for drama, but I supposed the police had to take the rumors seriously and act on the side of caution, despite the fact Jake wasn't even allowed to attend the burial.

Mama's best friends were tending to her and told me they'd take her home and get her settled.

A wake had been planned at my house with food, drink and music; all arranged by Nia's friends and extended family members.

By the time I got home my house was filled with people heating up food and arranging the back yard with chairs and tables. I was exhausted but they assured me they had everything under control.

I took off my heels and replaced them with flats, then went over to Ma's to check on Mama. She had already retired to her room and locked the door. She had been doing this since she moved up there from her house, so I wasn't worried.

I was thankful that the children weren't home. Their paternal grandmother had agreed to keep them until the next day.

Back at my place, the celebration of life had kicked in and it seemed that hundreds of people had shown up. Daddy made a speech and thanked everyone for being there. Someone said a prayer and then food was served.

I stayed inside, sitting at the kitchen table. At around ten o'clock, one of Nia's friends came to the kitchen door with a hat full of money. He said they'd taken a donation to assist the family in our time of need.

"Thank you," I said, but my mind whispered, *we're going to need something way more valuable than money to help us get through what's to come.*

I thanked him for his kindness. I understood the gesture as a part of our culture and the people's way of helping. I knew they didn't have any idea of what lie ahead for us. I wished it was as simple as having the funds to make it all better, to make this horrible nightmare go away.

Sadly, that was not the case.

Celebrate life
Not only after its demise
But Now
While it's alive

CHAPTER 12

Everything was moving so quickly, the police and the prosecution wasted little time in bringing this case to court.

Man admits killing brother

In Supreme Court yesterday, a 25-year-old man admitted killing his younger brother.

███████████, of Hamilton Parish, rejected murder charges but accepted a reduced charge of manslaughter at the monthly arraignments session.

███████ appeared calm and collected.

Chief Justice, the Hon. Mr. Austin Ward remanded him in custody until sentencing next month.

███████ was charged with the stabbing death of his 23-year-old brother ███████ following a Court Street brawl last February.

███████, a well-known moto-cross rider, died of his injuries at King Edward VII Memorial Hospital just before 3 a.m. on February 5.

● The man accused of an October shootout at the Spinning Wheel

On May 2, 1995, The Royal Gazette headline which read: *"Man Admits Killing Brother,"* was a sober reminder to everyone who had forgotten that this case was still ongoing; that the Cole family was still dealing with the reality of the death of their youngest son and the expected Supreme Court trial of their eldest.

It had been twelve weeks since Nia had been buried and the process threatened to reopen his casket with a long, drawn-out trial.

Jake came to everyone's rescue and pleaded guilty on May 1st, 1995, to a lesser charge of manslaughter. His plea negated the need for a trial and his sentencing was set for June.

In the same arraignment session, an accused shooter at the same nightclub pleaded not guilty to charges of attempted murder and four additional charges including unlawful wounding and use of a firearm. This incident happened in October, seven months prior. Only three months had passed since the incident between Jake and Nia.

They say that god's timing is perfect and most times we're not able to ascertain how the path we are on leads to anything good.

We didn't know it then, but Jake would need special assistance during the nights in prison. The gods had put everything in place to ensure he had the support only they knew would be required.

The Lord had said 'tend to his mind' and the events unfolded in such a way that someone close would be there to do just that.

Quickly! Urged the gods
There is life to be lived
Death has had its day

CHAPTER 13

"Jury finds man guilty of drug importation"
(*May 2, 1995*)
The Royal Gazette
"A Hamilton Parish man is to be sentenced on May 19 after a jury convicted him yesterday of importing and handling up to a quarter of a million dollars of marijuana intended for sale."

The day before these articles were published saw me running from one court to the other. Jake was in the court's monthly arraignment session, which was being held at the top of the hill on Parliament Street, and Daddy's case was in its final stages at the bottom of the hill on Front Street.

Jury finds man guilty of drug importation

A Hamilton Parish man is to be sentenced on May 10 after a jury convicted him yesterday of importing and handling up to a quarter of a million dollars worth of marijuana intended for **sale**.

███████████, 52, of Harlem Heights Road, was ordered held in custody to await sentencing by Puisne Judge the Hon. Mrs. Justice Wade.

In Supreme Court yesterday, a jury of four men and eight women unanimously found ███████ guilty of importing illegal drugs. And in a 10-2 decision, the jury also found him guilty of knowingly handling illegal drugs intended for supply on April 6, 1994.

Customs officers at Number 8 Shed discovered just over five kilograms of marijuana hidden inside one of 56 cases of Black and Tan beer imported by ███████ from the United States, Court was told during a trial last week.

In an undercover operation, Police replaced the case with a dummy package and dusted it with fingerprint powder.

A Police officer in civilian clothes followed the truck that collected the cases to Hip Hop Fashions boutique in Hamilton Parish where ███████ was arrested.

Depending on how the drugs were sold, they would have fetched between $90,000 and $255,000 on the streets of Bermuda, Court was told.

███████ maintained he knew nothing of the drugs. And his lawyer Mr. ███████ argued he was the victim of a conspiracy.

It was certain that Jake would be returning to the prison after the session ended. I had hoped that Daddy was found not guilty and he would be going home after the verdict had been rendered.

Sadly, that was not the case.

Daddy would be heading to the prison that day as well. The judge had remanded him in custody until his sentencing after the jury came back with a guilty verdict.

Mama and I were physically present but mentally, we were unaccounted for. We were in our own private worlds. I had no idea what she was thinking but my mind was all over the place.

At Jake's hearing, *I* was all but ready to plead guilty. I thought Mama and I both should have. The courts had missed it entirely. We were *all* guilty; guilty of creating, planning and executing the past events. They didn't know the history of our family. They didn't know how the boys had been raised and what they had witnessed – how Daddy had asked them which parent they wanted to live with when the divorce was final; how Mama made sure they were told constantly that their father was good for nothing; how I left them to fend for themselves.

I knew, and I wanted *everyone* to know: the judges, police, lawyers – all of them – that if Jake was guilty then we all were; that they had to set aside sentencing dates for us too. We should be required to enter an institution by the process of our admittance of failure to love and protect two minors under our care.

They should hear us out and listen to us recall the ways in which we played a major part in the facts revealed. But most importantly, this information would serve as proof that we were all to blame.

But this was not the job of the court system; it was something we had to deal with as a family. Collectively or individually, we would eventually all have to deal with our guilt.

I really felt that Jake shouldn't have to stand alone and solely take the blame for what had happened even though none of us were there that night. I was an emotional mess!

The two boys I had helped to raise and felt responsible for, one of them was now six feet under and the other was on his way back to prison, where he would wear orange every day. Our father would join him, he too wearing orange. I hadn't ever seen either of them wear this color as a choice and now neither of them had one in the matter.

The day's events left me completely drained. I didn't want to talk to anyone. I just wanted to go home and hold my babies. Holding them, an act meant to quiet my mind, had me questioning my ability to be a good mother. Once again, I started wondering what I could've done differently to affect Jake's and Nia's lives. I was like a mother to them and I was convinced I had done something wrong. Would I make the same mistakes with my own two?

I'd loved those boys, but I had left them.

I felt like I had failed.

I hoped that nothing like this would ever happen to my children.

They say be careful of your thoughts because they create your reality. My thoughts that day waited years to come to fruition but become reality, they did. My babies would require that I be there for them during the most traumatizing time of their lives because there would be another unexpected death of a close loved one. And their lives would forever be changed.

He never gives you more than you can bear
But our burdens have long been too much
Maybe it was we who filled our bags to the brim
And it had nothing to do with Him
That is,
Until we lay both bags and burdens down

CHAPTER 14

On May 19th, Daddy received a 7-year concurrent sentence for each charge of importing and handling up to a quarter of a million dollars' worth of marijuana.

On Friday, June 2nd, Jake was sentenced to 6 years for killing his younger brother.

In court he sniffled continuously and when asked if he had anything to say, he stood and said, "I apologize to my entire family and the community. Nobody could ever know how I feel right now. I really loved my brother." Jake broke down crying loudly and said, "I would give my life for his. I don't know what to do with myself."

At Jake's sentencing the Crown Counsel told the court that on February 4th, Jake Cole arrived at the

Captain's Lounge at 11 PM and joined his brother and other friends for drinks.

Shortly after 1 AM., they all went to the Spinning Wheel where the accused was searched by security personnel. A metal knife, approximately 8 to 10 inches long, was removed from his right boot and confiscated.

Between 1 and 2:45 AM, the accused and deceased were involved in at least three altercations requiring intervention by security.

He added that on the first occasion, the accused and deceased were found fighting, which included knocking over chairs and tables. After this fight, the accused told the deceased that he'd "get him" when they got downstairs.

Shortly after that, the accused came back upstairs carrying a knife in his hand. The accused threatened to cut the deceased, but he did not do so. This fight was also broken up.

Another fight occurred when the accused held a butter knife to the deceased's throat. This fight was also broken up and the accused was evicted from the club.

When he was leaving, the accused demanded the return of his knife, which had been originally confiscated. The security refused but did turn it over to a female accompanying him.

The lawyer continued, saying that the accused then forcibly took the knife from the woman and became involved with another altercation with his brother.

Man jailed for killing brother

█████████ was sent to prison for six years yesterday for killing his younger brother, 28-year-old █████████.

And right before the Chief Justice, the Hon. Mr. Justice Ward, sentenced him, the accused said tearfully: "Nobody could ever know how I feel right now. I really loved my brother."

As he broke down in tears while standing in the dock of the Supreme Court yesterday, the 25-year-old Spencer apologised to his family, friends and the community.

"I would give my life for his, I don't know what to do with myself."

On Thursday during arraignments in the Supreme Court, █████████ pleaded guilty to the reduced charge of manslaughter.

Mr. Justice Ward said he had taken all the mitigating factors into consideration.

"The death of any person in violent circumstances is a matter of public concern. On the night of his brother's death █████████ was carrying knives and he used one to produce a horrific assault. There are no words by him that will restore the life of his brother," he added.

Crown Counsel Mr. Brian Calhoun told the court that on February 4 this year, █████████ arrived at the Captain's Lounge at 11 p.m. and joined his brother and other friends for drinks.

"Shortly after 1 a.m. they all went to the Spinning Wheel where the accused was searched by security personnel. A metal knife approximately eight to ten inches long was removed from his right boot and confiscated.

"Between 1 a.m. and 2.45 a.m. the accused and the deceased were involved in at least three altercations requiring intervention by security."

Mr. Calhoun added that on the first occasion the accused and the deceased were found fighting which included knocking over tables and chairs. After this fight was broken up, the accused told the deceased that he would "get him" when they got downstairs.

Shortly after that the accused came back upstairs carrying a knife in his hand. The accused and the deceased fought again during which time the accused threatened to cut the deceased, but he did not do so. This fight was also broken up.

Another fight occurred when the accused held a butterfly knife to the deceased's throat. This fight was also broken up and the deceased was evicted from the club.

"When he was leaving, the accused demanded the return of his knife which had originally been confiscated. The security refused but did turn it over to a female accompanying him.

Blah, blah, blah read the article of the island's daily newspaper, The Royal Gazette. They had the responsibility of printing the Crown's case. Apparently, the public had a right to know.

I had no issue with what had been reported. It was exactly as it had been the day before in the Supreme Court, which was the first time I had heard any of what was being said. What I had an issue with was that it was all bullshit – lies made up by people who would not be identified.

The 'female' accompanying Jake especially angered me. What female? The security personnel had outright lied. They'd given the knife back to him!

I wondered just how effective these security officers really were in evading the violence that was occurring on our streets.

The punishments had an even bigger effect on me. Daddy had received two seven-year concurrent sentences for marijuana handling and importation versus Jake's six years for murder.

This was what they called justice.

And no matter what I thought or felt, this was the verdict by the Hon. Mrs. Justice Wade and the Hon. Mr. Justice Ward. There was nothing that could be done to change their conclusions.

Daddy and his lawyer Mr. Robles would later appeal the decision, but the sentence would be upheld.

With no other choice but to accept their fates, both men settled into their new lives as prison inmates as best they could.

After the sentencing it was difficult for Jake, and as Daddy recounted there were many nights Jake howled like a wolf. He said it could be heard throughout the prison. On these nights, the officers would allow him to be with Jake in an attempt to comfort him. It took some time, but he was eventually able to get through the nights on his own.

If there was a silver lining this would be it. They would both have each other for the majority of their sentences.

Our weekends became dedicated visiting time, seeing one at a time until we were able to see both simultaneously.

There wasn't much we could do to affect their lives on the inside other than to put the required twenty-five dollars on their canteen accounts at the prison for toiletries and treats like cigarettes and snacks and go to visit them.

I quickly made friends with other visitors and the inmates. Identifying the men that were in the same section with Daddy and Jake was easy; they all wore orange.

Larieka, who I had known previously, often visited her brother who was in the same section as both Daddy and Jake. We got to talking after one Sunday visit and she told me about another one of her brothers, a pastor, who had access to visit the men to share The Word and encourage them on a weekly basis.

She told me about the visits and what was involved, disclosing that she attended on occasion. Shortly after our chat, in which I expressed interest in joining them, I was invited to go with her and her brother as an assistant. I actually made it inside the prison with them on more than one occasion, but it wasn't long before prison officers recognized us from our normal visits and put two and two together.

They realized that Larieka and I were anything but religious teachers. We showed up one night as we had previously and were denied entry without explanation by the officer on duty. We were disappointed but chuckled as we sat outside the prison waiting for her brother to finish his studies with the men. We had a good run of it and we both knew that it would only be a matter of time. We were just two sisters who loved the men in our lives, even though they had made some life-changing decisions. We wanted to be there for them, even if we had to pose as ministers of

The Word. Neither of us was really into the god-being-our-savior stuff, but the opportunity presented itself and we took full advantage of it.

Getting to talk to the men on a more personal level allowed me to create lasting relationships. We had good laughs and insightful conversations but the horror stories of sexual abuse and drug overdoses that apparently happened inside of the prison kept me up at night. I could only hope that Jake and Daddy would be ok. Being able to see them outside of normal visiting hours brought me some relief and quelled my fears.

The men in maximum security became their own little family and as families do, they assisted each other. Their family members also helped in any way that they could. We would share our visitation passes. This allowed us to see our loved ones more often. I had become really close with one inmate who had been found guilty of a shooting. His mom and I would talk frequently, and we quickly became friends.

He was a brilliant character. He was funny and always had something to say. He decided that he would study law during his temporary stay at West-gate. He was making the best of his situation and even though he was physically in prison, he knew that they couldn't imprison his mind. His mind was as free as he chose it to be, and he used that freedom to his advantage; eventually earning his law degree.

Jake, on the other hand, appeared to be mentally imprisoned. He was made to attend weekly counseling sessions that only seemed to anger him. He said the doctor would constantly revisit the night of the incident without giving him any real direction on where he was to go next, leaving him to relive the night over and over again.

Mama tried to hire a private psychologist for him. I went with her to meet with prison officials who repeatedly denied her requests. They had a counselor on staff and saw no need to allow another to counsel Jake, no matter his special circumstances.

Jake was left with no choice but to attend the sessions within the prison and although he appeared to be acclimating to this new environment, we knew he wasn't getting the psychological help he needed.

Prior to being at Westgate Correctional, Jake was known to drink too much. He had displayed violent behavior before and each time he'd been intoxicated. I had no idea that alcohol was even available inside of the prison and was surprised when I learned that Jake was drinking again.

I asked Daddy about it and he said that Jake was cool, and not to worry.

So, I didn't.

———————

Three to four years later, they were both moved to the Prison Farm. The Farm was where you were sent when transitioning from incarceration to freedom. Even though they could be there for years, it was the facility meant to prepare inmates for living on the outside again. They were allowed work detail called Work Release. They would find jobs with the help of their families and were deemed responsible enough to leave the facility, go to work and return by the required time.

By this time, Jake was what I would describe as an outright alcoholic. The prison counseling at Westgate hadn't helped him to heal. Instead, he had resorted to drinking the prison-made alcohol. It had become his go-to remedy. The alcohol worked in a very different way. It numbed his pain. It allowed him to forget, if only for a few moments, and the prescription was not complicated. When it had worn off and the memories returned, you just needed to drink more.

I'm still baffled that the prison counselor did not pick up on this, or maybe he did, and it just made his job easier. I had always thought that the *system* had no interest in the rehabilitation of the inmates. And now at the Prison Farm, he was being afforded the opportunity to go on work detail. It was a freedom meant to assist with his re-acclimation to life on the outside, which I'm certain, was a daunting thought to him.

Having been locked up and only seeing the same people over and over again allowed him to escape the reality of what he had done, to some degree. He didn't have to face the hundreds of people he had encountered prior to being removed from society. He hadn't experienced people looking away when they saw him because they didn't know what to say. Or worse, have them staring at him without uttering a word. Understandably, some of these people were still angry and hadn't had the opportunity to express their feelings. I doubted any of them would actually tell him how they felt, but their looks of disgust would have the same effect.

I worried that life on the outside was not going to be a walk in the park for Jake, and I wondered how he would cope should any of those things happened.

He had already found a way to cope in prison and now that he had been granted some freedom, I was concerned that he hadn't been adequately prepared to deal with it all. Jake quickly decided that all he had to do was drink more and numb whatever feelings arose within him. Doing this made it easy for him to not give a fuck about the people who'd decided they didn't like him. He became friends with the bartenders and his daily work release quickly turned into drink fests. Many times, he would find his own way back to The Farm, as this was the protocol. The inmates had to show a sense of responsibility by getting themselves to work and back to the facility independently.

Most times, both Jake and Daddy took the bus back and forth.

We didn't generally break the rules, but there were times when Jake needed a ride back to The Farm and I would agree to take him. He would call me hours before he was due to return, and we'd agree on where we would meet. Most times I would pick him up near where he and Daddy had lived, the neighborhood we'd grown up in. He rarely ventured past Harlem Heights on most days, which made perfect sense to me. Jake had friends in the neighborhood. They were happy to see him and more than happy to share a drink or two. And it was where he felt safe and comfortable

Our old neighborhood was full of alcoholics. The house right next to ours was known as the drinking spot for the older men and they sat around all day drinking and sharing their experiences. It was an old, dilapidated house owned by one of the men. I always wondered how they could live like that. They were happy men, who had accepted their lot in life, which consisted of a roof over their heads and as much alcohol as they could consume.

There were lots of children in the neighborhood and most of what they saw growing up were older alcoholic men and younger men on drugs, not the best example of what a man could be, but it was what it was.

This was our homestead on Daddy's side. His mom lived above us and his brother and his family directly behind us; and of course, Uncle Grady was around the corner. It seemed as if everyone in our neighborhood was somehow related. We had so many cousins, aunts and uncles, and even if there wasn't an actual blood connection, they were considered our family anyway.

Jake had a loyalty to the family of the neighborhood. He felt welcomed there and it was no surprise that he would end up there or at the neighborhood cricket club most days he was on work release.

Jake did do odd jobs occasionally, but he somehow always ended his days there.

Daddy didn't seem to venture much past Harlem Heights during his work release either. He also had friends in the neighborhood and during his work release they would take him fishing, which was considered work. He couldn't sell the fish he caught but with his experience, he was certain to assist them with their overall catch for the day. He also found odd jobs cutting grass and manicuring yards in the neighborhood. He made time between jobs to go to his house and fix whatever needed to be fixed and maintain his yard as well.

I'm sure both he and Jake were bucking the system, but it seemed the system didn't care. Jake couldn't find work with a company, but he found plenty of odd jobs and most of them were in Harlem Heights.

The restaurant had been closed shortly after Daddy was locked up. The people who ran the club where the restaurant was located didn't want any association with a convicted drug importer, even though at one point they were his friends.

Burchall's Cove, where the boats were kept, was a short distance from the Prison Farm and it wasn't difficult for Daddy to go and spend a day on the water, weather allowing. He kept busy. He was eager to be permanently released without parole and was making sure he got his affairs in order for that day.

He tried to keep an eye on Jake but grew weary when Jake's attacks became more of a personal nature, directed at him.

Jake, with his newfound freedom, was drinking a lot more and when he was in a drunken state would become aggressive and nasty. The things he would say and his body language would become too much for Daddy to handle when they both were back at the Prison Farm and in their cells. There was no reasoning with him when he was in that state and Daddy decided to keep his distance, as his drinking had gotten increasingly worse. To my knowledge the prison didn't place Jake in a program or discipline him for his drinking or the behavior he displayed.

The two of them had their good days too. It was a very complicated and confusing relationship. Jake depended on Daddy when the nightmares haunted him in the dark and cold prison cell at night, although this didn't happen anymore, like it did when they were at Westgate. It was only when he was intoxicated that he acted as if he hated Daddy. It was almost as if he blamed him for what had happened and where he now found himself.

Despite the way Jake acted, Daddy always found a way to defend him, making allowances for his behavior even when it was directed towards him. They had a bond more than that of father and son. It was if they each had something on the other, something no one else knew about. As frustrated as Daddy was with Jake's behavior, he continued to defend him. The two of them had always been close but became even closer after Nia was born. Jake was Daddy's sparring partner. Jake was right in the middle of everything Daddy had gone through.

There was the night Mama drove with Jake and me in tow to Daddy's boat, certain he was there with another woman. We arrived at the square in St. George's, the boat was docked there and sure enough there was a woman onboard with Daddy.

Mama and Daddy started physically fighting. The woman ran away and Jake ran towards Daddy. I'm not sure what he thought he was going to do to stop them with his small self. I just stood, watching while screaming for them to stop.

Just then, Mama screamed. Jake, who had been behind Daddy had been struck with a paddle kept onboard the boat. Mama had picked it up and while Daddy was trying to take it from her, Jake had been hit in the face and was bleeding profusely.

Then there was the time when one of the men from overseas was visiting and Mama came home to find Jake with a white substance all over his face. The boy had been found face down in what was apparently a drug.

Jake and Daddy had shared some disturbing situations when Jake was still quite young.

Daddy, who was now a born-again Christian, had become very forgiving and seemed really hurt by the things Jake would say to him. He didn't understand that everyone wasn't like him. Not everyone found it easy to forgive or to forget.

Before they went to prison, and after Mama and Daddy had divorced, Jake lived with Daddy and Nia lived with Mama. I lived in the same neighborhood as Mama, just up the hill, and could always hear when there was an argument going on at her place.

On one rainy day, Mama had a leak in her house and called Jake to come and help her do something about it. Jake lived at least forty-five minutes away and had to ride his motorcycle to Mama's in the pouring rain only to find Nia lying in bed listening to music.

He was angry.

We both knew that she favored Nia, but this was too much of a direct slap in the face for Jake.

I heard him and Nia arguing and went down to see what was going on. It was easy to see how Mama saw Jake as the instigator but there was no way he would leave there without speaking his mind and asking Nia why he didn't get up to help Mama. The question that wasn't asked was, had Mama even ask Nia to assist her? Why would he have to ride that distance in the rain when Nia was there relaxing and was more than capable of fixing what was then her issue – a water leak?

Mama didn't see herself. She acted as if Jake owed her something, as if his choosing to live with Daddy was a crime against her, and it seemed that she was determined to make him pay for it.

Jake often found himself in situations like these. I'm sure it was easier for him to lash out at Nia. He had no idea of the conflict that was being caused by Mama's actions.

I saw that my brothers were being pitted against each other. I had seen the way they were being toyed with and I tried my best to get them to see it too. I tried to get them to see that they weren't at war with each other. I did my best to explain to them what went on between Mama and Daddy had nothing to do with them, but they each had different loyalties to our parents and there was no getting through to either of them.

Nia had a way with Mama. He was the only one she listened to, and he was the only one of us that could tell her how he felt without consequences. In his own way, he would tell her about something she'd said or done, he would speak in a very firm tone. In those days he would've been deemed disrespectful, but she listened to him and quietly reflected on whatever he had said. He was the only one who could literally leave her having nothing to say.

The boys each loved their parent of choice, always making it two versus two. Then there was me, standing somewhere in the middle.

The war that wasn't ours had been in full effect for years. Every war has its casualties, but this war had no winners.

We had all lost.

The alliances were tight, but none could've seen this coming. I don't believe my parents intended on this being the outcome at all: two boys at each other's throats with a point to prove to two parents who were always at each other throats, having a point to prove to the other. It wasn't clear what anyone's point was. What *was* becoming clear was that two brothers who loved each other very much were starting to hate one another, and their hatred was fueled by our parents' actions, whether it was intentional or not.

On this particular day, I picked Jake up at the bottom of the hill of Harlem Heights. I had pulled over in the bus layby directly across from the hill leading to our old neighborhood. Jake was stumbling as he crossed the street. I could smell the alcohol on him as he got in the car slamming the door.

"What?" he asked as I turned to look back at him. He always sat in the back seat; this was so no one would see him in the car. He was sweating and his face was red.

I didn't answer him. Instead, I turned around and started driving. His noisy breathing had subsided, and I glanced at him through the rearview mirror.

He seemed a bit calmer and was staring out the window.

"What did you do today?" I asked.

"What the fuck do you think I did? I drank!" was his response.

Well, that was pretty obvious, I thought.

"Listen, I am not the enemy," I responded. "I'm only trying to have a conversation with you. Do you really think all this drinking is helping you? Do you think it looks good for you when you go back to The Farm drunk? Aren't you worried about losing your privileges?"

Those were the worst words I could have chosen. I had unintentionally reminded him that he had already lost his freedom; that he had already lost way too much and now his behavior threatened to make him lose even more.

"You think I fucking care?" he shouted. "I don't give a fuck about those people. I am locked up because I killed Nia. Yeah, I'm an ass and I know that's what you think of me. I fucking killed him, and I'd do it all over again!"

His behavior startled me. I hadn't seen him like this in a very long time. We were on Ferry Reach Road and less than five minutes away from The Farm, so I pulled the car over. I turned to look directly at him. He glared at me and before I knew it, I had reacted in a way that wasn't typical.

"You can get the fuck out of my car and walk the rest of the way!" I said to him sternly. My tone was so low; I almost didn't recognize the sound of my own voice.

I was not only startled but I was angry too, and the words had a flow of their own. I wasn't normally an insensitive person, but I was so taken aback by what he had said.

Jake didn't move. He sat there with hunched shoulders and shuffling his hands in and out of his pocket. I looked out at the water and instantly saw the Prison Farm from where we were parked.

Jake slowly leaned forward and wrapped his arms around the headrest of the seat in front of him, pulling himself forward.

I sat back in my seat and turned towards him. He looked at me and continued his tirade. He looked evil – possessed even – and he had my full attention.

"You want to know why I said what I said?" he asked. "Nia was a punk ass. Yeah, I know everyone thinks he was an angel. Innocent my ass – fuck him! He would've let Pops go to jail for his dumb shit. Fuck him!" he repeated. "Didn't you wonder why he wasn't worried? He wasn't because he didn't think they could find Pops guilty for his dumb shit... fucking ass. I told him to step up and just be honest, but nah, he was a sissy who thought everything was gonna be alright. Fuck, fuck, fuck!" he shouted. "And you all wonder why I drink? All he had to do was own up to his shit. Pops didn't know anything about that shit, but he had to be the fall-guy for his dumb ass. Out acting all bad, putting his hands on me like I ain't know what he done? I didn't want this shit to happen, but your boy didn't want to do right, so fuck him and fuck those people over there." He glared across the water at the Prison Farm. "I don't give a fuck 'cause everyone thinks I'm the bad one, but they don't know. They just don't know."

I was stunned and silenced by Jake's revelation and looked at the water as if it held the answers to what my next steps should be.

The ocean had always brought me peace, but as I stared at it that day, there was none to be found. The only thing I could see were the waves rolling and crashing on the rocky shore.

Damn, I thought. *Jake had just confirmed what the lawyer had alluded to years ago. Nia was responsible for the shipment of marijuana all along.*

Jake stopped talking and we sat in silence for about two minutes, and then suddenly, he began mumbling incoherently and sobbing.

I reached back to touch his shoulder as a gesture of compassion, but he pulled away. Having no idea what he was thinking, I thought it best to take him back to The Farm. Was it guilt or did he feel he had taken justice for Daddy? Or maybe he was just mad that he and Daddy were both locked up and he really believed that it was Nia's fault.

I thought the alcohol helped him to forget but now I wasn't so sure. Was this something he could ever forget? My mind was full of competing thoughts and questions like: did Daddy know?

Looking at the clock and realizing it was past his curfew, I started the car and began driving.

On this day, I let Jake out closer to the gate than I normally would have. Typically, I'd stopped further away, but I wanted to be certain I'd actually see him go inside.

He opened the door to get out and to my surprise he said, "Thanks Sis. I know I said a lot back there. I just had to get it off my chest. Thanks for hearing me out. I appreciate you."

Jake seemed sad, speaking with a much softer tone than he had just a few minutes ago. His actions were so chaotic and I had no idea what to make of any of it.

I reached back and grabbed his hand before he got out of the car. "I love you," I said affectionately.

"Love you too, Sis." he said as he closed the door and walked the short distance to the gate.

The officers let Jake inside and I drove off.

It would take me about forty-five minutes to get home depending on traffic. I tuned the radio to FM 89.1 for some easy listening music and made my way home.

The music wasn't as distracting as I had hoped.

I thought about what Jake had said. Now it made sense why he had acted the way he did the day Daddy was arrested; why he had treated Nia the way he had. I shook my head to dispel the thoughts. I started thinking it was because he was drunk and he was just running his mouth. Then I remembered that he hadn't been in the lawyer's office that day when Mr. Robles had mentioned the possibility of Nia being involved. How could he have known? I wondered if Mama had said something to him, but quickly let that go because I was certain that she wouldn't do anything to mar her favorite child's name.

Did daddy know the truth? Had he made the sacrifice of his life by going to prison for a crime he didn't commit? Who were these people I called family and how many secrets were they all keeping? What was I supposed to do now?

I wondered if I should tell anyone what Jake had revealed to me. I had so many questions, no answers and there was absolutely no one I could ask.

Damn my family.

and this time
you have to let it burn
your attempts to smother
little fires everywhere
resulted in rapid oxidation
it's an uncontrollable blaze now
let it burn
you can't put this one out
ashes to ashes dust to dust

CHAPTER 15

I didn't tell anyone what Jake had said to me that day. It haunted me and with the alliances still strong, even though Nia was no longer with us, I didn't know if either of my parents would believe me. Or if specifically in Daddy's case, he was already aware. If he did, then he didn't want me to know because he would've said something by now.

I continued to visit Jake and Daddy at the Prison Farm. I felt it was my duty and I would go there to find them mostly in good spirits unless there had been a disagreement between the two of them. On those occasions, Jake would not be in the visitation hall on time. He always straggled in halfway through the visit as if he felt he had to show up.

Jake's drunken disclosure wasn't discussed and I left well enough alone. During the visits we chose not to talk about either man's crime; instead, we found other ways to entertain each other, we'd talk about my children and how they were doing. If they'd come along, the entire time would be spent playing with them – coloring or drawing something.

One could only ask, "How are you doing?" so many times. It was evident that, although not the best of circumstances, the men were doing ok. They had made friends inside and Daddy had taken to tending to the prison garden and other inmates' issues, as if he didn't have enough of his own. That was just who he was. I understood that he believed by being there for others afforded him space from dealing with his own pressing issues, and if only for a little while, it was worth it to him.

Jake was a lot like Daddy. He was always helping someone else when he was able; when he wasn't drunk.

Mama also visited and was mostly concerned about Jake's wellbeing. At first it would be awkward sitting at the table with both her and Daddy, but Daddy would always break the silence by asking how she was.

"Doing as best I can," was almost always her response and I could hear the disdain in her voice. I think we all could, but we had learnt to ignore it.

I had become an expert at making uncomfortable situations more comfortable for everyone involved, and during those times I would always mention the garden or one of the kids' accomplishments. A recall of a sports day got everyone laughing at whatever it was one of them had done.

I silently wished we could talk about what had happened and how we planned to deal with it. I wanted to discuss what we would be like after they were released and what life would be like for the family. I wanted to know how everyone *really* felt, but those things weren't talked about. My family had gone straight into denial modus operandi and the reality of what had happened between Jake and Nia wouldn't be faced until Jake was officially released from prison and back at home with Mama.

Mama had started preparing for his release and was building an apartment for him next to hers, which ironically was also next to Nia's old room. I didn't think it was the best idea, but even if I had said something to her it wouldn't have mattered. She had her reasons, and nothing would've changed her mind.

I was troubled – worried that Jake hadn't received enough counseling to be released, that he would be even more detrimental to himself (and maybe even Mama) once he regained his freedom and was living next to her. None of what I thought would make a difference. Mama wanted her son to be at home, close to her.

Mirror, mirror on the wall
Just this once
Show us our agendas

We all did our best to resume our normal activities and as the years passed, we settled into what had become our new normal. Mama's new normal was a dark, depressing space and as much as I tried to make things a little easier for her, she wasn't ready to let go of all that had happened.

I would talk to my hairdresser about my challenges with Mama, and she would remind me to be patient with her.

"Zavane, your mama has been through a lot. Most women wouldn't have survived what she has. I think she's a brave woman. I know I wouldn't have been able to handle what she's been through."

I couldn't begin to imagine having to go through what she had either, so I remained patient, but it was hard. She had not ever treated me kindly and was still judgmental of whatever I chose to do or say. I loved her but had no idea how to show her that I did. I don't remember us hugging or saying those three words to one another. The past events did little to nothing to bring us closer. I had tried for years to prove that I wasn't her adversary, but instead, her little girl.

Mama was always asking me to do something for her or to take her somewhere and I would always oblige, thinking that maybe, just maybe this time she would realize I was really making an effort to be there for her, that she would reciprocate my efforts.

Jake would soon be released and living next to Mama. It would be good if she could get the help, I thought. She needed to at least try and get herself in a better mindset before Jake came home. For years she had treated Jake and I pretty much the same and I couldn't begin to imagine what their relationship would be like if she remained this way, especially with him being so close to her.

It might be rough for them, I thought.

Jake also needed counselling just as badly, if not more than Mama did. This had the potential for being catastrophic. Or maybe I was just overthinking everything.

One evening, at Mama's request, I had taken her for a drive. As had become the norm, it was a somber experience. Full of hope, I told her about this book I'd read where a woman had lost all of her children to a house explosion. She had survived because she'd run to her neighbor's house to ask them to call for help. The woman had shouted to her eldest child to get themselves and the other two children out, but they didn't make it in time and the house went up in flames just as she reached the neighbors door.

I suggested to Mama that she could be grateful that she still had two children who were living, but she just stared at me blankly.

I parked the car in my yard but before we got out, I calmly called to her, "Mama," and when she looked at me, I said: "I'm tired of being in this space with you. I don't know how long you intend to stay here, but from now on you are on your own because I can't stay in this space with you anymore."

She offered no response. Mama just opened the car door and walked the short distance next door to Ma's house as if I hadn't said anything to her.

Not knowing what she was thinking, I questioned my actions and wondered if I was being selfish. I walked into my house and was greeted by my children, and I knew that I had done the right thing for me and for them.

Shortly after that car drive, I decided to give up my way of thinking and follow in everyone else's footsteps. I figured I couldn't beat them so I would join them. I would no longer impose my thoughts on them about getting themselves or Jake the help I was convinced they needed. If everyone else thought they were fine, then so would I.

Although no one ever spoke of forgiveness, it appeared that they had all forgiven Jake. My thinking that it should be said and heard was too much to ask, I concluded. I gave them the benefit of the doubt because I wasn't really sure if forgiving was something you said or something you did, and to my knowledge both Mama and Daddy had chosen the latter. I too would show Jake I'd forgiven him, just like they did. Who was I to think that there was any other way to go about mending what had been broken so badly?

I thought they were foolish for sweeping this whole situation under the rug, but that's what we did. No matter the mess, we showed up as if nothing had happened. And even in the wake of this disaster, they would not change how they went about doing things.

I started to see a counselor to talk about my feelings, my fears and my family. It still perplexes me that I had to pay someone to listen to me, but I needed that.

I needed someone to tell me that I wasn't crazy; that my thinking that we couldn't fix this using the same methods that created it weren't far-fetched; that we had to change our behaviors in spite of what it looked like to everyone else.

But I had been groomed to perfection; domesticated as they say. I would express my true feelings with my counselor and resume putting on the persona required to be with my family.

I was no longer the little girl who related to Cinderella waiting for a prince to save me.

I was being strong by letting go of what I couldn't control and saving myself.

Don't touch the fire for it will burn you
Look both ways before you cross the street
Always be aware of your surroundings
But when the advisors become the ones that
threaten your very existence
Go within
For they have taught you well
And the time has come to use their advice
On them

Five people, one house
Living together
Each trying to survive
Each willing themselves to get out alive
Together yet very much alone
In the place they call home

CHAPTER 17

Daddy was in Agape House. There was nothing more that could be done for him other than to keep him as comfortable as possible.

He had battled prostate cancer for thirteen years and he was tired. He shared a room with two other men and although he didn't feel his best, he did all he could to be helpful to them. He spent most nights staying awake and keeping watch over one of his roommates, ringing for the nurse at any sign his friend needed them.

My birthday was coming, and I took vacation from work to enjoy the week on the beach and relax. There are no mistakes in this universe, for that week was the week Daddy took a turn for the worse and instead of lying on the beach, I spent my days and nights at his bedside.

I made a bed out of the visitor's chair and the room of three became a room of four. Every time Daddy had a visitor, he would start saying that this person or that said hello or that he had just seen them. I would ask the visitor who he was talking about and each time they would tell me the person in question was deceased. I felt that these transitioned souls were preparing him, letting him know he would not be alone.

I would wait until Daddy awoke in the morning and had what he needed before I left to go home and get a shower, then I would return and spend the day with him.

I took a break on my actual birthday, June 6th. My good friend Deanna insisted that I take some time to go and have dinner with her at one of the local restaurants on Front Street. I would be less than five minutes away from Daddy should he need me, so I agreed to go.

It was a quiet celebration. I always enjoyed spending time with Deanna. She had a very soothing effect on me, and her invite was timely. I needed the outing more than I was willing to acknowledge. I hadn't planned on doing anything celebratory. Daddy needed me and being by his bedside was more important.

On the morning of June 10th, after a night of watching the fishing channel with Daddy and having had the most uncomfortable sleep since staying there, I got up out of my makeshift bed, stretched and proceeded to make sure he had water, juice and something to eat before I left.

I didn't immediately shower that morning when I got home like I had become accustomed to doing. Instead, I made a cup of coffee and had not been sitting for very long on my balcony when I had one of those random thoughts telling me to go back to the hospice.

I had learnt a long time ago to pay attention to those strange thoughts that often entered my mind. So, without knowing exactly why, I made my way back.

As I was parking the car my phone rang. It was Dr. Alani. She was saying that Daddy was ready and that his spirit was fighting hard, he was holding on, but I needed to get back.

I told her I was in the parking lot and would be right in.

Daddy was in a completely different state than when I had left less than an hour ago. He was now unconscious. Damn, we had just talked, I thought. It was still early – 7 AM, and I didn't want to call anyone that early. In hindsight, I guess I knew I had time.

Sitting at his bedside, I took his hand in mine, placed my other hand on his heart and started chanting, "*Nam-Myoho-Renge-Kyo,*" my Buddhist mantra. I was a bit relieved because it was something I had wanted to do with him for a while, but he always had so many visitors, it became an impossible task to accomplish.

Nam means to devote or dedicate oneself. *Myo* is translated as mystic or wonderful. *Ho* means law. *Renge* means lotus blossom and *Kyo* literally means *sutra* and this mantra indicates the Mystic Law, the fundamental law that permeates life and the universe, the eternal truth. To chant *Nam-myoho-renge-kyo* is an act of faith in the Mystic Law and in the magnitude of life's inherent possibilities.

I believed that my chanting would help Daddy transition peacefully.

Daddy had different beliefs and we had discussed my beliefs in depth during the quiet times, when visitation was over and before he went to sleep. He was open to hearing what I believed in and was happy to know that I wouldn't ever consider him dead, but that I would think of him as simply having transitioned to another form.

I didn't realize that two hours had passed until my stepbrother Danez arrived, stopping by on his way to work. It was almost 9 AM and Daddy's condition hadn't changed. Grateful that he was there, I advised him of what the doctor had said and asked him to sit with Daddy while I went outside to make the necessary phone calls to the rest of the family.

By noon, there were about thirty people present. Most of them sat outside, with a few at his bedside at any given time. I sat in the garden outside Daddy's room on the grass with a direct view of his bed. I didn't want him to be alone, not for one minute, so I kept an eye on that.

People were coming and going and offering their sentiments and I talked to the visitors, leaving my immediate family members to their thoughts and feelings. This death was a private thing and I respected that and left them alone.

I was thanking one of Daddy's close friends for coming by and glanced in the room when I noticed it was empty. I said goodbye and hurried in and assumed my position from that morning.

Holding his hand with the other placed on his heart, I immediately felt the difference in his heartbeat; it was a lot slower. I resumed chanting. I'm not sure how much time had passed, but I soon noticed that his heart was skipping beats for longer periods of time. I raised my head from the bowed position opened my eyes and looked directly into his face. To my surprise, his eyes opened and he was now staring right back at me. We were nose to nose and I whispered to him that it was ok, that he would be fine and so would we. I told him I loved him. We continued looking into each other's eyes for what felt like forever. My hand was still holding his with the other still resting on his chest.

His eyes closed and then slowly his heart beat three more times and stopped.

Still looking at him, I said, "Thank you. That was beautiful."

I wasn't aware of anyone else in the room and when I looked up, I saw that his bed was surrounded with the family members and his room was full.

"I'm sorry," I said instantly, feeling that they wouldn't understand why I was thanking him when he had just left us.

Someone pressed the buzzer for the nurse. The doctor came and officially pronounced him dead.

Planning Daddy's funeral was easy compared to Nia's. The family met at my aunt's and quickly gathered the information for the obituary. Danez and I met with the funeral directors and selected a casket.

I was writing the obituary when I remembered a scene that had taken place at Agape House.

One of Daddy's friends from church came to visit and at that time; Daddy was still talking and had asked for a drink.

"Water or juice?" those of us in the room asked.

Daddy responded with a very clear and loud, "No."

My stepsister Nandi, my cousin Dace and I were convinced that he wanted an alcoholic drink. We were talking amongst ourselves and having a good laugh about our thoughts.

Daddy's friend didn't find our conversation funny at all. He turned to us and told us that there was no way Daddy had been asking for an alcoholic beverage. He had changed his ways and didn't indulge in drink anymore.

The three of us looked at each other after being so sternly scolded, and we couldn't help but burst into laughter.

Daddy's friend once again turned to look at us as if we were toddlers acting out of order.

I decided to add this incident to his obituary as a way of showing all aspects of the man I called Daddy.

Once I had it all typed up, I sent it to the graphic designer who was creating the program for the service.

Two days before the funeral, I went to collect the program and have a read over. I realized that the part about that day had been removed. I called the designer and questioned why it had been removed and all she said was that she could put it back in. I ignored the fact that she didn't answer my question and told her not to bother as we didn't have any time to do that.

I had a plan. I had the original copy and I would read from that one instead.

Excerpt from obituary:

"I want to thank the visitor who sternly reminded a few of us at Agape House that Daddy was no longer the man he used to be, and I want to leave you with a message today. Life and death are two different sides of the same coin. Oday used to always say, "You gotta take the good with the bad."

While each of us in this church today knew a different aspect of his life, I think we would all agree that he did just that; took the good with the bad. He always kept his head up and by god's grace; he always made it through whatever he was dealing with at the time. He was a selfless man who was always there for someone else. Even in his most difficult times, he would put on a brave face and tried his best to help those in need. It was hard to give to a man who always gave to others; it was hard to see his pain when he lost his sons, his brothers, his mom and best friend, Sam. Even during those times, he kept his head up and found someone in that situation who needed his help more than he needed anything we were trying to offer him.

Even his prison sentence gave him a new mission in life. Once again, it wasn't about him. He was there for his son, and he humbly accepted that as another one of the Father's plans for his life. He saw the bigger picture.

His experiences on the one side of the coin that was his life laid the foundation for the other side. The side that shows him back in church, becoming a deacon and his love for the Lord being expressed in just about every conversation he had.

You see, Oday figured it out early and always said, "You gotta take the good with the bad and you cannot have one without the other." Only by spending much time away from the church would he have known it was time for him to return. We ourselves wouldn't know light had we not experienced darkness but what he taught us was to not shun the darkness – to take it in stride, to keep our heads up and just do what we've got to do because the light was certain to come.

I finished by thanking Mama for choosing him to be our Daddy then returned to my seat in the front pew. The pastor was up next to deliver the eulogy. He closed his notebook, stood and went to the pulpit.

After a short prayer he began talking about Jesus and the disciples. "When Jesus was looking for disciples, he didn't look for the rich men; he didn't look for the distinguished man, no." His voice bellowed throughout the church. "He looked amongst the fishermen! And everyone knows that men who make a living of fishing are men with foul mouths, they are men who indulge in drink. They are not what one would call, refined men."

He continued. "We are here today to celebrate the life of one such man. A man who might've been considered lowly in life, ha! Yes, he had made mistakes, but as a fisherman he could learn new ways of doing things. Did you know that fishermen are some of the most teachable people on earth?" He asked the congregation. "Our brother Oday was a fisherman and God knew he would be able to use him later on in his life. And not only to spread His Word, but to be a catalyst to others who would follow in his footsteps and return to the ways of our God."

The pastor had everyone's attention and I was in complete awe of how he tied his message into what had been written in the obituary. He wouldn't have had a copy of the program ahead of time and besides, the part of Daddy wanting a drink wasn't in there.

The rest of the funeral went as planned. After the church service it had been arranged for Daddy to be taken on one final boat ride. The family met at the dock in St. George's and the men lifted his casket unto the ferry tugboat for Daddy's final ride on the ocean.

He was laid to rest in the Seventh Day Adventist graveyard close to Nana.

Change is the only constant
We must each one of us
Be prepared for change
Of both life
and death

CHAPTER 18

One could say that Jake had lost all of the men closest to him. He hadn't stopped drinking and at this point, I would argue that he couldn't. One could reason that the alcohol now controlled him and his drinking was no longer about what he had done years ago. He had lost two people who, at one point in his life, were very dear to him, and I'm certain that he wouldn't have ever thought that he'd ever have to choose between the two of them or that he himself would ever have to question the amount of loyalty he had for either; but in his mind, Nia's actions gave him no choice.

He had been thrown a curve ball. He had gotten caught up in the war that wasn't his and he had come out the victor, just by the sheer fact that he was the only one of them still alive. It could be assumed that his drinking was a clear indication that he wished that same death upon himself.

Although, I couldn't imagine that he wanted this for himself.

I have always believed in the saying 'As long as there's life, there's hope,' and Mama and I had been hopeful. We were optimistic that he would eventually forgive himself for his wrongdoings and that he would put the past to rest and start to live with the memories of a time when Nia and Daddy were here with us, and everyone got along. Like when we spent holidays on Daddy's boat swimming and fishing, or when we had family gatherings at Mama's poolside restaurant. Memories like traveling to Atlanta for motor-cross, the good times had been few and far between, but we had them.

Jake has other plans. He has learned how to get through each day, how to smile and get enjoyment out of his life; and although he continues to silence his demons in drink, he gets by.

Like he said in the intervention, "I like me. I'm happy being this way."

If happy means drowning out the thoughts that remind us of our iniquities, then Jake is as happy as he can be, as long as he has access to alcohol.

What is the point of living if you can't be happy, especially with whom you've become? I couldn't imagine walking in his shoes and who am I to judge his footsteps? I was just happy that he was still alive and had long given up being concerned about the shoes he chose to journey in. He really appeared to accept who he had become.

Nothing is the same in our family. Our already small family became smaller and more distant, but we do our best to stay in touch with each other. A phone call every so often between Jake and me is the way we keep in touch. Our calls always end with an "I love you." from both of us.

Jake and Mama see each other quite often. They still disagree on Jake's lifestyle but it's definitely a lot less volatile now.

Mama still expresses frustration at Jake's drinking, and she hasn't given up trying to help him get better either. If I had to guess, I'd say that she lives for the day he becomes sober.

It can't be easy to have to look into the eyes of the person who murdered your son, to be there for them and love them anyway, but Mama does it all the time.

A Mother's Prayer
Why Me?

The Lord answered and said: "Because you, my child, can handle it. Because you, my child, are strong, resilient, forgiving, and most of all, loving. Because the faith I have in you to show others the way cannot be thwarted by even what seems the worst that could ever happen. You, my child, are the chosen one and what a special one you are. It will be hard, very hard, but always know that I am with you every step of the way. You, my special child, are never alone."

Mama is living proof of the Lord's response.

She's another example of what a mother's love looks like.

Mothers are spiritual beings too, and yet mostly they are only ever treated like mothers.

Love suffers much
But it always wins
And
Winning
Is relative

CHAPTER 19

Jake has been ill, and the doctor has given him six months to live. After hearing this from our cousin, I call Jake being careful not to mention what I had been told. He says that he needs to talk to me, that he's got some bad news but would prefer to talk to me in person.

I ask if I can come by this upcoming weekend and he says no, he'll be going to the motor-cross track to watch the races, but he will let me know when I can.

He doesn't call about us meeting but he does call to inform me that he is checking himself into rehab. It's a two- to three-week program and he feels that it's time. This is something he wants to do, he says, and I suspect that whatever the doctor told him at his last visit is the reason behind his decision.

This is the very first time he has decided to enter rehab voluntarily and he sounds eager to go through the process and create a much-needed change in his life.

He doesn't sound afraid, but I imagine he is. I am happy for him, and I believe that this time, he might just go all the way and stay sober.

SEPTEMBER 2018

Jake is drinking again.

He calls first thing in the morning on every holiday. The last time I got a call was the Thursday morning of the Cup Match holiday. He wanted to know what we had planned; the answer is always 'nothing.' As a family, we had never been big on celebrating holidays; instead they're mostly viewed as a much-needed rest day.

He goes on to ask how everyone is doing. He asks about each family member individually, as if he's checking off a list and he remembers each of us. I can feel his smile through the phone as I go down the list of the latest happenings for every member of my household.

He tells me what he has planned for the day, and he *always* has something planned, even if it's just chilling in the yard to having a barbeque for the neighbors.

He always extends an invitation. I think he is just being polite with no real expectation for us to come.

I don't usually attend.

We get by on the pleasantries in our monthly catch ups and I do visit on occasion. On the odd occasion, Jake will come to our end of the island for a visit and he makes sure that he sees and speaks directly to everyone who is at either Mama's house or mine; we still live next to each other.

When I ask him how he is doing, he does his best to be positive with his responses. He might mention his latest setback, like not being able to find work, but there's always someone he plans to call for work the next day. He speaks with an intentional enthusiasm about this new possibility. I'm not sure either of us really believes that the opportunity will pan out. Most haven't to date, but I encourage him to follow up and make the call any way.

Sometimes, I hear the sadness in his voice when he talks about the uncertainty of his future, and every so often I can hear the fear. I let him know I understand by being just as intentional with my kind words and offers of support, proposing to update his resume or make a call on his behalf.

He has been through so much and although he hasn't thrived, he has certainly survived. With the pride instilled in us so long ago, it isn't easy to just lie down and surrender to defeat.

Jake has survived a broken neck and living in a head to waist cast for months. He has survived being the middle child and all the quirks that come with being born in that awkward position. He has survived murder charges and jail time. He has survived disapproval from people who he thought were supposed to love and support him no matter what he had done – unconditionally. He has survived losing the two men who were most important to him, one by his hand, the other to cancer and he has survived the war that he really had no choice but to be a participant in.

Jake has survived a life full of adversity and still wills himself to find a sliver of happiness in each day he wakes up to. And maybe the drink makes that possible, but I'm inclined to believe that it comes from a place deep within, a place where the truth resides, a place where the alcohol doesn't reach. It is in this place that he remembers who he really is.

And no matter what people say or think, that place remains intact, hopeful and happy. It keeps him holding on.

His spirit is reminded of who he is to *Be* every time his name is called: A *Strong Boy*. He had certainly lived up to the meaning of his name; there was a time when he had been more dapper, athletic and sharp. He's more rough and rugged now, but my god, he is still strong!

ON THE BRINK OF INSANITY

EXCERPT

Death would consume my family for years to come and I thought that the worst I would have to experience had passed until the evening I got the call that my children's father had drowned.

The morning of September 24, 2002, my daughter's 14th birthday, she had awakened crying, having had a dream of someone dying. She didn't know who it was, but she knew that she was on a hill facing the water where the person had died.

Later that evening, my two children, a childhood friend of my daughter's, Mama and Ma were at a restaurant waiting for their dad to show up when I called them to come back home.

I told Mama that there had been an accident, trying not to alarm her knowing that she would react emotionally and scare the children.

She persisted in knowing what had happened and she screamed when I told her. As I knew would be the case, the children were alarmed. I could hear them in the background asking her what was wrong, their little voices full of fear.

I paced as I answered my phone, call after call from friends wanting to know if I had heard the news.

I didn't know what I was going to say to them. How was I supposed to tell them that their dad was gone?

That man always knew how to get to me. This time he had outdone himself.

My daughter's life would by no means be the same. She would spend years punishing herself for not returning her dad's phone call earlier that day because she was certain she would see him later that night.

'*On The Brink of Insanity*' will take you through her struggles, triumphs and her own bout with self-medicating substances.

If you have enjoyed the Cole family saga you will want to read all about the Bells.

'On The Brink of Insanity'

Coming Soon!